OUR LIFE WITH JESUS

OUR LIFE
WITH JESUS

Faith and Life Series

Third Edition

BOOK THREE

Ignatius Press, San Francisco
Catholics United for the Faith, Steubenville, Ohio

Nihil Obstat: Reverend James M. Dunfee
                  Censor Librorum
Imprimatur: + Most Reverend Bishop R. Daniel Conlon
                  Bishop of Steubenville

Director of First Edition: The late Rev. Msgr. Eugene Kevane, Ph.D.
Assistant Director and General Editor of First Edition: Patricia Puccetti Donahoe, M.A.
First Edition Writer: Therese Vorndran Nichols
Director and General Editor of Revision: Caroline Avakoff, M.A.
Revision Writer: Colette Ellis, M.A.
Revision Artist: Christopher J. Pelicano

Catholics United for the Faith, Inc. and Ignatius Press gratefully acknowledge the guidance and assistance of the late Reverend Monsignor Eugene Kevane, Director of the Pontifical Catechetical Institute, Diocese of Arlington, Virginia, in the production of the First Edition of this series. The First Edition intended to implement the authentic approach in Catholic catechesis given to the Church through documents of the Holy See and in particular the Conference of Joseph Cardinal Ratzinger on "Sources and Transmission of Faith". The Revised Edition and Third Edition continue this commitment by drawing upon the *Catechism of the Catholic Church* (Libreria Editrice Vaticana, © 1994, 1997).

The Subcommittee on the Catechism, United States Conference of Catholic Bishops, has found this catechetical text to be in conformity with the *Catechism of the Catholic Church*.

2015 reprint
See www.faithandlifeseries.com
for additional tools and resources
© 1987, 2003, 2011 Catholics United for the Faith, Inc.
All rights reserved
ISBN 978-1-58617-565-8
Manufactured by Friesens Corporation
Manufactured in Altona, MB, Canada, in March 2015
Job # 210773
in compliance with the
Consumer Protection Safety Act

Contents

A Note to Parents

Dear Parents,

The *Faith and Life* series was originally published in 1984. The book you hold in your hands is one of over 4.6 million books sold since then. From the beginning, the series was intended to provide schools, parishes, and families with the catechetical tools and essential elements of Catholic doctrine pivotal in the formation of young Catholics.

While the doctrines and Tradition of the Church remain essentially unchanged, as time has passed the editors have provided additional teaching tools that enrich the series and make it even more accessible to all types of students. Since its introduction, the series has seen the addition of activity books, teacher's manuals, numerous online resources, scriptural quotations, and correlations with the *Catechism of the Catholic Church*. Additionally, this edition has been updated to incorporate the new translations of the Roman Missal introduced into the Mass during Advent 2011.

In this third grade student text, *Our Life With Jesus*, you will find that emphasis has been given to the scriptural basis of our Faith in accord with Sacred Tradition. Every chapter opens with a Scripture passage, and important verses supplement the text where relevant. Each chapter closes with questions and answers based on Church teaching as found in the *Catechism of the Catholic Church*. Vocabulary words are indicated in bold type and in the Words to Know sections. Their definitions are found in the glossary. Common Catholic prayers are also taught in the lessons, and presented at the end of the book.

It is important to realize that, as parents, you are the primary educators of your child. Your active participation in your child's religious education is highly encouraged by the Church. As a family, you are the first witnesses of God's love to your child. If you provide a model of Catholic living at home, if as a family you participate in the sacramental life of the Church, and if you pray and attend Mass together, your child is more likely to take to heart the lessons he will learn in religion class. Family discussions of current events with a healthy religious perspective will allow your child to grow up with a better understanding of the world around him, and more importantly, help him to be a true Catholic and follower of Christ in the midst of it. As stated in the *General Directory for Catechesis*, "family catechesis precedes . . . accompanies and enriches all forms of catechesis" (GDC, 226; Congregation for the Clergy, 1998). Providing your child with a strong Catholic identity at an early age, while not ensuring a lifetime of devotion, will certainly prepare him for the challenge of becoming a faithful Catholic adult.

We encourage you to use the *Our Life With Jesus* student text, along with its resources, to assist you in the task of sharing the Good News with which you have been entrusted. More information and resources can be found at www.faithandlifeseries.com.

We sincerely hope that this series will provide parents, catechists, and teachers with the assistance they need in the task of evangelizing young people.

1   God Loves Us

"O give thanks to the LORD, for he is good,
    for his mercy endures for ever.
O give thanks to the God of gods,
    for his mercy endures for ever.
O give thanks to the Lord of lords,
    for his mercy endures for ever."

Psalms 136:1–3

Did you know that God has lived for ever? Close your eyes and imagine billions and billions of years ago. God was alive. He existed before time began. Now imagine billions of years stretching into the future. God will still be alive. God is eternal, which means He had *no* beginning and He will *never* die. He is all powerful, all holy, all wise, and **all perfect**. His love and mercy are **infinite**. That means they are far too great to be measured.

God was thinking of you, loving you, and wanting you from all eternity. Long before He put one star in the sky, He knew you. He knew your name. He knew your face. He knew the color of your eyes and the sound of your voice. You are very precious to Him. He could have made some other person, but He wanted you. So He made you just the way you are.

God loves you so much that He made you in His image. He made a part of you that, like Him, will never die. This part of you is called your soul. It is a spirit. You cannot see it. Because you have a soul, you have the power to think and the power to love. You can also learn things, enjoy music and stories, talk, and laugh. Without your soul, you would be no more intelligent than a rock. Without your soul, you could never love anyone. When God made us in His image, He opened up many treasures for us.

Our greatest treasure is God Himself. He is always with us. He knows everything about us: who we are, what we do, and even our thoughts. He loves us far more than anyone else loves us. He gave each of us a soul so we could love Him in return. Sometimes this seems hard to do because we cannot see God, since God is pure spirit.

There is only one God, but in God there are three Divine Persons: God the Father, God the Son, and God the Holy Spirit. Jesus is God the Son. He is the Second Person of the Blessed Trinity. He came to earth as a sign of God's love for us. Because Jesus, Who is God, became a man like us, it is easier for us to know and love Him. We know that He is gentle, kind, and good. He taught us to put God first. He taught us to obey God, even when we do not feel like it. He taught us that by loving each other, we give glory to God and show our love to Him.

Jesus taught His Apostles—and us—how to pray to our Heavenly Father. Sometimes Jesus went out into the desert to pray. This showed us that it is good to take special times to be alone with God. Other times, Jesus prayed with a gathering of friends or a great multitude. We follow His example when we pray with our family or classmates or others in our parish.

Once the Apostles asked Jesus how to pray. He taught them a prayer that is still used in our Church. We hear it every time we go to Mass. It is called the Our Father or the Lord's Prayer:

Our Father, Who art in Heaven, hallowed be Thy Name; Thy Kingdom come; Thy will be done on earth as it is in Heaven. Give us this day our daily bread, and forgive us our trespasses as we forgive those who trespass against us; and lead us not into temptation, but deliver us from evil. *Amen*.

In this prayer we praise God, we say we are sorry for our sins, we ask for His love and forgiveness, and we ask Him to watch over us. **Prayer** is talking with God. It is important to pray every day because it keeps us close to Him.

Words to Know:

all perfect   infinite   prayer

Q. 1   *Who created us?*
God created us, body and soul, in His image (CCC 704–5).

Q. 2   *What purpose did God have in mind when He created us?*
God created us to know Him, to love Him and to serve Him in this life, and then to be happy with Him forever in the next life, in Heaven (CCC 358).

Q. 3   *Who is God?*
God is the all-perfect pure spirit. God is three Divine Persons: God the Father, God the Son, and God the Holy Spirit (CCC 202, 307).

Q. 4   *What does "all perfect" mean?*
"All perfect" means that every good is found in God, without defect and without limit. In other words, it means that He has endless power, wisdom, goodness, and love (CCC 41, 213).

Q. 5 *Does God have a body as we have?*
No, God does not have a body, for He is a perfectly pure spirit (CCC 370).

Q. 6 *Where is God?*
God is in Heaven, on earth, and in every place: He is the unlimited Being (CCC 300, 326).

Q. 7 *Has God always existed?*
Yes, God always has been and always will be: He is eternal (CCC 212).

Q. 8 *Does God know all things?*
Yes, God knows all things, even our thoughts: He is all knowing (CCC 216, 2500).

Q. 9 *What is prayer?*
Prayer is talking with and listening to God (CCC 2559–61).

Q. 10 *What is the Our Father?*
The Our Father is the prayer Jesus taught His Apostles to pray. We still say this prayer today (CCC 2759).

2 God Created the World

"In the beginning God created the heavens and the
earth. The earth was without form and void, and
darkness was upon the face of the deep; and the Spirit
of God was moving over the face of the waters."

Genesis 1:1–2

In the beginning, there was only a great darkness. There was no
earth, no light, no people, or animals, or trees.

God was perfectly happy, so He did not need to create these things.
But in His infinite goodness and love, He wanted to share His life. So
He created all of Heaven and earth.

Creating something means making it out of nothing. When a
carpenter makes a chair, he cannot do it without his hammer, nails,
and wood. When a baker makes a cake, he cannot do it without eggs
and sugar and milk. But God **created** the world, which means He
made it out of nothing. Only God is so powerful that He can make
something just by thinking of it and willing it to be.

First God said, "Let there be light!" and the sun and moon and
millions of stars brightened the sky. Then He created the sparkling sea
and the land. He put birds in the air and animals of all shapes and
sizes on the earth. Finally, God made a man and a woman in His own
image and likeness. They were Adam and Eve, our first parents. God
made them to know, love, and serve Him by loving and helping each
other, ruling the earth, and enjoying its beauty together.

Everything that God created is good. We believe in God's wisdom
and love because everything in nature has a purpose. For example, a
porcupine's funny needles are not for decoration. God planned them

ait dieux ror rourel rel ch

so that a porcupine could protect himself from danger. A mother kangaroo's pouch is not an accident. God planned that soft, warm place to keep her babies safe.

The things in nature work together. When a bee takes food from a flower, his legs get full of pollen, which is needed for little flower seeds. As he flies away, the pollen scatters so lots of new flowers will grow. God made the mountains tall so they can catch snow. Then the snow high above the ground melts slowly and trickles down to water the earth all year.

We believe that God is the **Lord**, or master of all things. It takes a brilliant plan to make all of nature work this way. That is why we believe it comes from God.

God has a purpose for you, too. He created you to one day be happy with Him in Heaven. He also created you first to be a part of this world. At Baptism He gave His life, called grace, to your soul. He gave you talents to serve His Kingdom. He gave you five senses, so you can see, hear, taste, touch, and smell the beautiful things on this earth. Naturally, God wants you to enjoy these gifts and be happy.

Only one thing ruins His plan for our happiness: **sin**. When we sin, we do not use God's gifts in the way He wants us to use them. When we sin we do not feel right inside. We feel wrong and upset. We turn our backs on our loving God.

God gave us our mind and will so we can choose to live His plan for us. We can choose to do what is right and good. When we obey our parents, study well, are kind to our neighbors and friends, and respect animals and nature, we please God. We feel right inside.

To be happy forever, we must get to Heaven. **Heaven** is our greatest hope. God promises He will take us there if we love and serve Him in this world. We will be completely happy forever in Heaven because we will see God face to face. We are not sure what

Heaven looks like, but we know it will be even more beautiful than we can imagine. God gave us His word: "What no eye has seen, nor ear heard, nor the heart of man conceived, what God has prepared for those who love him" (1 Corinthians 2:9).

Words to Know:

create   Lord   sin   Heaven

Q. 11 *Does God take care of His creation?*
Yes, God takes care of His creation. He keeps all things in existence and directs all of them toward their own purpose with infinite wisdom, goodness, and justice (CCC 301–2).

Q. 12 *Can God do all things?*
God can do all that He wills to do: He is the all-powerful one (CCC 268).

Q. 13 *What does "Creator" mean?*
"Creator" means that God made all things out of nothing (CCC 296).

Q. 14 *What does "Lord" mean?*
"Lord" means that God is the absolute master of all things (CCC 450).

Q. 15 *What ruins God's plan for our happiness?*
Sin ruins God's plan for our happiness (CCC 1847).

3   Learning about God

"This is eternal life, that they know you the only true God, and Jesus Christ whom you have sent."

John 17:3

We believe God is with us because He gives us many signs of His presence. One of the best signs is the world all around us. Everything in nature acts for a purpose. It has order, and it has great beauty. Even a person who has never heard about God can figure out that Someone very wise and powerful must have put nature together. The different parts of creation give us many clues about God, our **Creator**.

Mountains and vast forests reveal that our Creator is majestic and great. Oceans and rushing waterfalls tell us of His power. Fresh roses and sunsets reflect God's beauty. The growth and seasons of living things show us that God is wise. And the company of good, loving people teaches us more about God's own goodness and love.

God made sure we had many ways to discover Him, since He created us to know and love Him. Long ago, before the coming of Jesus, God sent messages to His people through holy men called prophets. **Prophets** were men who prepared the people for the coming of the Savior. Moses, for example, was a great prophet. Through Moses, and other Old Testament prophets, God taught mankind to be good, to stop sinning, and to trust in Him.

God later revealed Himself to us more directly through Jesus Christ, His Son, our Savior. Remember, Jesus is God the Son, the Second Person of the Blessed Trinity. His way of life on earth showed us what God is really like. We learn through Jesus that God is gentle as well as just, slow to anger, rich in mercy, and full of love. We learn that He

18

forgives the greatest sins if we are sorry for them. We learn that He is always ready to heal us, help us, and be our friend.

Jesus often taught these things through parables. **Parables** are stories about ordinary people that teach us something about the Kingdom of God. Each parable is different, but they all teach one clear message from God: "Love God with all your heart and soul and might, and love your neighbor as yourself."

We find Jesus' parables and other things He said and did in a big book called the Bible. The **Bible** is the holy book God gave us. It has two parts, the Old Testament and the New Testament. The **Old Testament** is the first part of the Bible. It teaches us about Creation, our first parents, and the long wait and preparation of God's people for the Savior. The **New Testament** is the second part of the Bible. It tells the story of Jesus and how the Church began. It teaches us that the Church is our ladder to Heaven.

God inspired holy men from earliest times to write down His Law and teachings. These are recorded in the Bible. That is why we call it the Word of God. We also call it Scripture. God's teaching was also passed on through words and deeds that weren't written in the Bible. That teaching is called Tradition. Scripture and Tradition teach us everything we need to know to live a good and happy life that is pleasing to God.

Jesus, our Teacher, once called Himself the Good Shepherd because He watches over us and leads us to the Father. After Jesus left the earth, He gave us another shepherd to take His place. We call this shepherd the Vicar of Christ or the **Pope**. The Pope teaches and guides the Church for Christ. He encourages us to become saints. He is the head of the **bishops** all over the world. He helps them in their mission to help us keep learning and growing in our Faith.

Words to Know:

Creator   prophet   parable   Bible
Old Testament   New Testament   Pope   bishop

Q. 16   *Can we know about God from the world around us?*
Yes, we can know about God from the world around us. God's goodness, wisdom, power, and beauty can be seen in His creation (CCC 34).

Q. 17   *Does creation reveal all we need to know about God?*
No, creation cannot reveal all we need to know about God, so God chose to reveal Himself through prophets and, later, through His own Son, Jesus Christ (CCC 35, 50, 65).

Q. 18   *How could Jesus reveal God to us?*
Jesus could reveal God to us because Jesus is God the Son. He taught us about God through His life, actions, and words (CCC 65, 2763).

Q. 19   *Does the Bible contain all we need to know about God and His plan for men?*
No, the Bible does not contain all we need to know of God's Word, but Scripture and Tradition as taught by the Church show us everything we need to know about God (CCC 67, 78, 80).

Q. 20 *How can we be sure that the Church teaches us the truth about God and His plan?*
We can be sure that the Church teaches us the truth because Jesus founded the Church and established Peter as the first Pope. Since then, all Popes and bishops are helped by God to guide and teach all people the truths of God (CCC 85–86).

HIC EXPVLIT ADA 7 EVA DE PA
DISO DS 7 POSVIT CHERVBIN C
TODE CV FLAMEO GLADIO

22

4   The Promise of a Savior

"The LORD God said to the serpent,
'Because you have done this,
   cursed are you above all cattle,
   and above all wild animals;
upon your belly you shall go,
   and dust you shall eat
   all the days of your life.
I will put enmity between you and the woman,
   and between your seed and her seed;
he shall bruise your head,
   and you shall bruise his heel.'"

Genesis 3:14–15

God made other creatures, besides man, who have the power to know and to decide. These creatures can think as we do, but they are much smarter and more powerful. They are called angels. We cannot see the angels because they are pure spirits. They have no bodies. But they are very real and alive, because God shared His life with them, too.

God created the angels out of love. He wanted them to be happy with Him in Heaven for ever. He gave them the gift of free will so they could choose to love Him in return. Some of the angels chose to rebel against God. They refused to serve God.

The bad angels and the good angels fought a great battle. The good, obedient angels won because they had God and the truth on their side. God rewarded them with the joys and love of His Kingdom. Then God sent all the bad angels (devils) into Hell. They can never see God again because they locked themselves out of Heaven when they chose to rebel against Him.

Like the angels, Adam and Eve were given free wills. They were created to be God's friends forever, but they had a choice. God tested that choice. He told Adam and Eve to enjoy all the fruits of their rich, beautiful garden, except for the fruit of one tree. He warned them that if they ate this fruit, they would die.

One day, however, the devil tricked Eve by lying to her. He told her that if she disobeyed God, she would not die, but would be like God. Eve believed the devil and ate the forbidden fruit. Then she gave some to Adam to eat too. This first sin was called **Original Sin**. Since Adam was the father of all people on earth, the effects of his Original Sin carry on to all generations, including our own, and to each one of us.

When Adam and Eve disobeyed God, they were worried, sad, and full of fear. They lost the gift of His life in their souls. They could no longer please Him or be His friends. Worst of all, they had to suffer and die.

God punished Adam and Eve, but He never stopped loving them. He planned a special way for them to come back to Him after their Fall. He promised a Savior, Who would make up for their sin and re-open the gates of Heaven, which were closed by Original Sin. This promise became the light and hope of the People of God.

Jesus died on the Cross to make up for our sins. He is the **Savior** of the world. He rose from the dead gaining God's eternal life for us. He wants us all to share this life, so He gave us the Sacrament of Baptism. **Baptism** pours God's life back into the soul, washing away Original Sin. When the priest poured the waters of Baptism over you, you shared in Jesus' death and Resurrection. You were born into God's family. God came to live inside of you. Because of your Baptism, you are able to go to Heaven someday.

You can keep your soul full of **grace** (God's life within us) by obeying and loving God. Jesus' death on the Cross teaches us that no matter how attractive a sin might appear, it is never worth the price. Sin makes us sad and afraid, and it hurts our friendship with God. Obedience and love make us happy, and they strengthen our friendship with God. If we keep our souls full of grace, we will one day rejoice with God in Heaven, our true home.

Words to Know:

Original Sin   Savior   Baptism   grace

Q. 21 *What is sin?*
Sin is an offense done to God by choosing to disobey His Law (CCC 1849).

Q. 22 *What is Original Sin?*
Original Sin is the sin committed by Adam and Eve. Every person receives this sin from Adam and Eve, our first parents (CCC 404).

Q. 23 *How is Original Sin taken away?*
Original Sin is taken away by God's grace given in the Sacrament of Baptism (CCC 405).

Q. 24 *Why is man able to go to Heaven?*
Man is able to go to Heaven because Jesus paid the price for our sins by His suffering and death (CCC 598, 601).

5 Abraham: The Father Of God's People

"By myself I have sworn, says the LORD, because you
have done this, and have not withheld your son, your
only-begotten son, I will indeed bless you, and I will
multiply your descendants as the stars of heaven and as
the sand which is on the seashore. And your descendants
shall possess the gate of their enemies, and by your
descendants shall all the nations of the earth bless
themselves, because you have obeyed my voice."

Genesis 22:16–18

The people who lived after Adam and Eve waited a long time for
the promised Savior. Some of them got tired of waiting and made up
their own gods. They worshiped great things in nature that they could
see, like fire, the moon, and the sun. They even worshiped objects
they made with their hands, like animal statues made of gold.

These people forgot God, but God did not forget them. He
remembered His promise to send a Savior. But first God chose certain
faithful men to prepare the people for the coming of the Savior.
Abraham was one of the first He chose. Abraham had a great gift
from God, called **faith**.

God asked Abraham to leave his home and friends and go on a
long journey. Abraham did not understand clearly, but because of
his faith he believed in the one true God. Also because of his faith,
Abraham trusted God. **Trust** means to depend on and hope in
someone. Abraham took his wife, Sarah, his nephew Lot, and all his

flocks to a faraway country called Canaan. God rewarded Abraham for his obedience. He told him, "This land I will give to you. You shall be the father of a great people. Through you all nations will be blessed." Because of this promise, this land was called "the Promised Land." Abraham did not realize it, but God's plan was that the Savior would be born from his family.

God was very good to Abraham. He gave him great riches and increased his flocks. But Abraham was worried because he had no children. When Abraham and his wife, Sarah, were very old, God blessed them with a child. They named the boy Isaac, which means "laughter," since he was such a surprise and delight in their lives.

One day God tested Abraham to see if he loved Him above all else. He knew Isaac was more precious to Abraham than any other treasure. One night God said to Abraham, "Take Isaac and go to a mountain that I will show you. There offer Me your son as a sacrifice." Abraham's heart was breaking, but again he put God first. He trusted and obeyed Him. He cut wood for the sacrifice, took Isaac, and walked up into the mountains. Just as Abraham was about to strike his only son, an angel sent by God stopped him. "God now knows that you truly love Him," the angel said, "for you are ready to obey Him in all things. God is pleased with you. He will bless you even more."

Abraham was very glad. He picked up a ram which was caught in the bushes and sacrificed it in thanksgiving. Then the angel told Abraham that his family would be more numerous than the stars in the sky. He told him that out of this great people, God's Chosen People, the Savior of the world would one day be born. God gave this great reward to Abraham and his children because Abraham always obeyed His voice, even when God asked him to do something very hard.

Some day God may test us as He tested Abraham. He may ask us to give up something we love or want in order to follow His commands. This happens in small ways every day. God asks you to obey your mother right away, even though you would rather keep playing. God asks you to be kind to everyone, even people who have hurt you. God asks you to follow His Laws, even when it would be easier to follow another way. God has happiness and blessings in store for your love and obedience, just as He did for His faithful servant Abraham.

Words to Know:

Abraham   faith   trust

Q. 25 *Did God send a Savior right away?*
No, the people who lived after Adam and Eve waited a long time for the Savior to come (CCC 65).

Q. 26 *How did God prepare the people for the coming of the Savior?*
God chose faithful men like Abraham to prepare the people for the coming of the Savior (CCC 51, 53).

Q. 27 *How did God prepare Abraham?*
God called Abraham to leave his home and friends to go to the Promised Land. God blessed him with riches, animals, and a beloved son (CCC 59).

Q. 28 *How did God test Abraham?*
God asked Abraham to sacrifice his beloved son, Isaac, to see if Abraham loved God above all else (Genesis 22:1–12).

Q. 29 *Did Abraham pass God's test?*
Yes, God saw that Abraham was faithful and obedient. God told Abraham that his descendants would be many, and that the Savior would come from his family (CCC 59).

6 The Prophet Moses

"God said to Moses, 'I AM WHO I AM.' And he said, 'Say
this to the sons of Israel, "I AM has sent me to you."'
God also said to Moses, 'Say this to the sons of
Israel, "The LORD, the God of your fathers, the God of
Abraham, the God of Isaac, and the God of Jacob, has
sent me to you": this is my name for ever, and thus I am
to be remembered throughout all generations.'"

Exodus 3:14–15

As God promised Abraham, the Chosen People grew and
multiplied like the stars in the sky. They spread across the land as a
great and powerful people. Night and day, God watched over them
and blessed them, for He loved them as His own children.

Sometimes God tests the people He loves the most. This happened
to the Israelites in Egypt. They were God's favorites, His chosen ones,
but God allowed them to endure a long, dark period of suffering to
test their faith.

It all began with a selfish **Pharaoh**, or king of Egypt. At first, one
Pharaoh had welcomed the Israelites into Egypt. But later another
Pharaoh grew jealous of their loyalty to the one true God. He also
grew afraid of their great numbers and strength. He decided to control
God's people by making them his slaves. Then he commanded that
every one of their newborn sons be thrown into the river, so the
Israelites would not be a danger to the Egyptians.

God's people were confused and full of sorrow. But God never left
them. He made a plan to set His people free. He chose an Israelite
called **Moses** to be His special helper. Moses' mother was able to save

32

him from the Pharaoh's cruel command by putting her baby in a small basket woven of papyrus and hiding him among reeds of the river. It was the Pharaoh's daughter who discovered the child and took him home to the Egyptian palace. Moses grew up with the royal family, but he always knew he was an Israelite.

One day God spoke to Moses from a burning bush. He told Moses, "I hear the cries of My people. I know that they are suffering. Come now! I will send you to Pharaoh to lead My people, the Israelites, out of Egypt." At first Moses was afraid. He made many excuses. But finally he agreed to go because God promised him, "I will be with you and I will help you. Trust in Me."

Moses went to the Pharaoh as God commanded. "Let my people go!" he said. Moses warned the Pharaoh that he came in the name of God. The Pharaoh just laughed. He ignored Moses and treated the Israelite slaves even more harshly. God punished this cruel king by sending many plagues, or disasters, to his land. All the water in Egypt turned to blood. A huge number of frogs and bugs covered the crops and houses. Hailstorms swept across the land. Terrible illnesses hurt the Egyptian people. The country was plunged into darkness. Each time Pharaoh cried, "Stop this plague! I will let your people go!" But time and time again, the Pharaoh broke his promise. He had no intention of setting his slaves free.

Finally, God sent the most terrible plague of all. He sent the Angel of Death to kill the firstborn of every Egyptian home. The Israelites were spared this tragedy because they obeyed God's command that each family share a special meal after killing a lamb and sprinkling the lamb's blood on the doorposts of their houses. When the Angel of Death saw this sign, he passed over the house and it was safe. This was called the Passover. Therefore, only the Egyptians lost their firstborn children. The Pharaoh was so full of grief, he finally gave in. He let the Israelite people go.

Moses led the People of God out of Egypt to safety. The escape was full of danger, for soon the Pharaoh changed his mind again and ordered his army to chase them. God protected His children by parting the Red Sea so they could cross it. Then God closed the water, and it swallowed up the Pharaoh's men.

God protected the people in many more ways during their long journey to **Canaan**, the Promised Land. He gave them bread called manna and fresh water from a rock. He encouraged them when they were tired or losing hope. He invited Moses up to a mountain-top to receive Ten Commandments that would make His people holy and happy. Over and over again God lived up to His promise, or **covenant**: "You will be My people, and I will be your God."

The God of Abraham and Moses is our God. There is only one true God. He still speaks in our hearts today: "You will be My people, and I will be your God."

Words to Know:

Pharaoh   Moses   Canaan   covenant

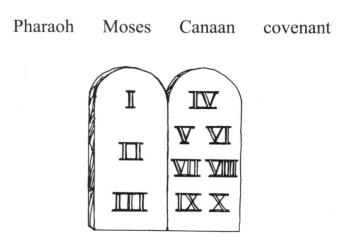

Q. 30 *How did God save Moses as a baby from the cruelty of Pharaoh?*
Moses was saved from Pharaoh's cruelty when his mother placed him in the river. Pharaoh's daughter found Moses and took him into her home, according to God's plan (Exodus 2:1–10).

Q. 31 *How did God speak to Moses?*
God spoke to Moses in a burning bush (Exodus 3:2–4).

Q. 32 *Why did God send the plagues to Egypt?*
God sent the plagues to Egypt to show that He is the true God, and to punish Pharaoh for not freeing God's Chosen People from slavery (Exodus 10:1–2).

Q. 33 *What is Passover?*
Passover is the celebration of the night God's Angel of Death passed over the houses of the Israelites, whose doors were marked with the blood of a lamb (Exodus 12:23, 27).

Q. 34 *How did God care for His people on their way to the Promised Land?*
God gave His people the manna to eat and water from a rock to drink. He encouraged them to continue on their journey (Exodus 16:21, 17:6).

7   God's Laws of Love

"For it is not the hearers of the law who are righteous before God, but the doers of the law who will be justified."

Romans 2:13

After the children of God had safely escaped Egypt, they still had challenges to face. They had a long way to go before they reached the Promised Land. God had protected them on their way. He gave them quail meat, a bread-like food called manna, and fresh water from a rock. He gave them enough each day to satisfy their hunger and thirst.

God also wanted to nourish the souls of His children. He wanted to teach them how to love Him and be good to each other. One day, God called Moses, His prophet, to the top of **Mount Sinai** and gave him the rules of His Kingdom. We call these rules the Ten **Commandments**. God gave them to Moses written on stone tablets, but He wants them to be written on our hearts.

The first three Commandments told the people how to worship and respect God. The last seven told them how to be kind and fair to each other. The Commandments asked them to do some things and avoid others. God meant all ten of these to work together in our daily life. He also meant them to bring happiness and joy to His children's lives. He wanted to protect them from the sadness of sin.

Even though God gave the Ten Commandments to His people during the time of the Old Testament, they are meant for all God's people until the end of time.

When some people asked Jesus which of the Commandments was the greatest, He answered:

"You shall love the Lord your God with all your heart, and with all your soul, and with all your mind. This is the great and first commandment. And a second is like it, You shall love your neighbor as yourself."

Matthew 22:37–39

Keeping God's Commandments is not always easy, but they are for our good. They help us to love God and our neighbor. Some day we will see God face to face. If we have followed His Commandments on earth, He promises to share with us the joys of Heaven that last forever.

THE TEN COMMANDMENTS

1. I am the Lord your God; you shall not have other gods before Me.
2. You shall not take the name of the Lord your God in vain.
3. Remember to keep holy the Lord's Day.
4. Honor your father and your mother.
5. You shall not kill.
6. You shall not commit adultery.
7. You shall not steal.
8. You shall not lie.
9. You shall not covet your neighbor's wife.
10. You shall not covet your neighbor's goods.

Words to Know:

Mount Sinai   Commandments

Q. 35 *What are the Commandments of God?*
The Commandments of God are the moral
Laws that God gave to Moses on Mount Sinai
for all His people (CCC 62, 2056).

Q. 36 *Must we follow the Commandments of God?*
Yes, we must follow the Commandments of
God (CCC 1776, 2072–73).

"If you love me, you will keep my commandments."

John 14:15

40

8   King David

"Your house and your kingdom shall be made sure for
ever before me; your throne shall be established for ever."

2 Samuel 7:16

Many years after the Israelites escaped from Egypt, they decided
they wanted to have an earthly **king** like the other nations. God
warned them against having a king, but since the Israelites really
wanted one, He said yes. God told the holy prophet Samuel to
anoint the new king by pouring oil over his head. Anointing was a
sign of God's gift of power.

A man named Saul was chosen to be the king of Israel, but Saul
turned out to be weak and disobedient to God. Therefore, God chose
another king named David to rule over His people after Saul died.
David was only a young shepherd boy, but he turned out to be a very
great and wonderful king of Israel. He was a kind and strong leader,
talented and clear-thinking in battle. He conquered Jerusalem and
made it the city of his people. Best of all, King David really loved
God. Sometimes he fell into sin, but he was always sorry and came
back to God. He helped his people to lead good lives.

David teaches us about God's presence in our lives and His love
for us. David also teaches us how we should love God in return. God
was faithful to David by helping him win a victory over the cruel
champion Goliath. **Goliath**, who challenged the People of God, was
over nine feet tall and carried a heavy metal sword. David, who stood
up for the People of God, was small and had no sword. We would
think that the boy David would not have a chance. And yet, David
trusted God enough to fight Goliath, and he won. David showed his

people that even when all hope seems lost, God is near us. God's strength and help are more powerful than anything else in this world.

King David taught us the importance of prayer, or talking with God. David used his beautiful voice and musical talents to make up songs for God. These Psalms, which are messages of praise and love, are still sung in the Church today, many centuries later. We sing them or read them at Mass because the words that David sang so long ago still express the same things we believe today: God is mighty and beautiful. His mercy is everlasting. We trust and love and adore Him. We are sorry for sin. We delight in the treasures of His creation. We thank Him for sharing His life.

David was a good king and God promised that the Savior, the eternal King, would come into the world through his family. David, in fact, foreshadowed the Savior in many ways. Like Jesus, David was a good shepherd who took care of his flock. He was a wise and just king. He was willing to lay down his life for his people when he saved them from Goliath. He listened to the Father. David, the poet-king, was a hero in God's plan to save mankind.

Words to Know:

king   anoint   David   Goliath

Read this Psalm from the Bible and listen carefully to the words. Why do you think King David's poems are still so important today? Can you make up a prayer of praise in words of your own?

The Lord is my shepherd,
  I shall not want;
  he makes me lie down in green pastures.
He leads me beside still waters;
  he restores my soul.
He leads me in paths of righteousness
  for his name's sake.

Even though I walk through the valley
   of the shadow of death,
  I fear no evil;
for you are with me;
  your rod and your staff
  they comfort me.

You prepare a table before me
  in the presence of my enemies;
you anoint my head with oil,
  my cup overflows.
Surely goodness and mercy shall follow me
  all the days of my life;
and I shall dwell in the house of the Lord
  for ever.

Psalm 23

Q. 37 *How could David prepare God's people for Jesus?*
David could prepare God's people for Jesus
because David was a shepherd who took care of
his flock, like Jesus the Good Shepherd. David
was a wise and just king. He was willing to lay
down his life by fighting Goliath for his people
(1 Samuel 16:11–17).

Q. 38 *Why was David anointed with oil?*
David was anointed with oil as a sign of his
authority to be a king chosen by God (1 Samuel
16:12–14).

9 Loving God Most of All

"And you shall love the LORD your God with all your heart, and with all your soul, and with all your might."

Deuteronomy 6:5

Our God is so holy and magnificent that we can never love Him too much. He is our Creator and King. He is also a loving Father Who cares for us more than anyone else in the world can. We cannot see God, but He is with us all the time. Everything we have is a gift from Him. He gave us our life, our family, our beautiful world, and many other gifts.

Because God is perfect and can do all things, we give to Him something that we do not give to anyone else. We adore and worship Him. We pray to Him, believe in Him, hope in Him, and love Him. The angels also praise and adore God. They appeared to shepherds in Bethlehem when Jesus was born, singing, "Glory to God in the highest, and on earth peace among men with whom He is pleased."

God Himself told us in the First Commandment, "I am the Lord your God. You shall not have other gods before Me." In this Commandment, He asks us to know that He is the one true God and to love Him above all things.

The "other gods" that God told us not to worship are everyday persons, places, or things that can lead us away from Him. Some examples might be money, pleasures, toys, or nice clothes. These things are good and we can enjoy them, but we must not let them take our attention away from God. The things of this earth will pass away,

45

46

> "O LORD, our Lord, how majestic is your name in all the earth!"
>
> Psalm 8:9

but God is for ever and He has destined us to live with Him for ever. Nothing on earth can compare with God and the treasures that He gives. That is why He comes first.

God does not want us to be superstitious. To be **superstitious** is to believe in or trust in something other than God. This would insult our Lord instead of giving Him glory.

The Second Commandment is: "You shall not take the name of the Lord your God in vain." We are only to use the name of God to speak to Him or about Him in a **reverent** or loving way.

People in the Old Testament knew how great God is, so they were very careful when they spoke His name. When Jesus came to earth, He encouraged us to call on God's name often. He taught us a prayer that we still say together at every Mass. "Our Father, Who art in Heaven, hallowed be Thy name. . . ." Hallowed means holy. The name of God is holy and it has power. We know this because the Apostles worked many miracles in Jesus' name. Jesus promised, "Whatever you ask in My name will be done."

The name of Jesus is just as powerful today. If you are lonely or afraid, call on Jesus' name. He will come to you. If you are confused or have a problem at home or at school, call on Jesus' name. He will help you. Jesus hears us every time we call. At Benediction, we praise Him for this by joyfully saying, "Blessed be God. Blessed be His holy name."

The Second Commandment also tells us to **respect**, or think highly of, holy places and things. A church is a holy place. When we go into

47

a church, we can show love for God by quietly listening to the priest and obeying our parents. We can turn to Jesus in the tabernacle or look at the image of Jesus on the crucifix, and we can pray. We should genuflect and make the Sign of the Cross when we enter or leave. God will bless us for these acts of love.

Whether we are in a church, a park, our home, or a car, we can always praise God. We can tell Him silently or quietly that we believe in Him, hope in Him, and love Him most of all.

A Song of Praise:

HOLY GOD, WE PRAISE THY NAME

Holy God, we praise Thy name!
    Lord of all, we bow before Thee.
All on earth Thy sceptre claim;
    All in Heaven above adore Thee.
Infinite Thy vast domain,
    Everlasting is Thy reign!

Q. 39 *What does the First Commandment, "I am the Lord your God; you shall not have other gods before Me" tell us to do?*
The First Commandment tells us to believe in God and to love Him, to adore Him, and to serve Him alone (CCC 2084).

Q. 40 *What does the First Commandment tell us not to do?*
The First Commandment tells us not to put anyone or anything before God. This means we are not to be impious, superstitious, or irreligious. Also, we must not deny the truths taught to us by the Church (CCC 88, 2110).

Q. 41 *What does the Second Commandment, "You shall not take the name of the Lord your God in vain," tell us to do?*
The Second Commandment tells us to keep the name of God holy, and to honor the vows and promises we have made (CCC 2142, 2147).

Q. 42 *What does the Second Commandment tell us not to do?*
The Second Commandment tells us not to use the name of God without respect, blaspheme God or the most holy Virgin, the saints, or holy things. We also must not swear oaths that are false, unnecessary, or wrong in any way (CCC 2150, 2155).

Words to Know:

superstitious   reverent   respect

10   The Lord's Day

"This is the day which the LORD has made;
let us rejoice and be glad in it."

Psalm 118:24

When God created the world, He worked for six days and on the seventh He rested. God values the work we do, but He wants us to take one day of the week to rest, too. He also wants us to use that day to join others in worship. In the Old Testament, God's people stopped working and gathered together for worship on the Sabbath, or Saturday. However, the early Christians rested and came together to rejoice on Sunday because Jesus, our Lord and Savior, rose from the dead on Easter Sunday morning.

We still keep Sunday as a special day to celebrate the miracle of the Resurrection. God is very pleased when we do this because His Third Commandment to us is, "Remember to keep holy the Lord's Day."

The greatest gift that we can offer to God on His day is to go to Mass faithfully. At every Mass, we give ourselves to God and join ourselves with Christ's gift of Himself to the Father. The Father in turn gives us His own Son as "the Bread of Life," Who nourishes our souls. This makes Sunday not only a day of praise but also a day of blessings and joy.

Holy Days of Obligation (such as Christmas, All Saints' Day, the Feast of the Ascension, and the Feast of the Immaculate Conception) are considered just as special as Sundays. They are days we mark as celebrations or feasts of special worship. God wants us to keep those days holy, too, by praying, going to Mass, and not working.

Sunday is not only a day of worship but also a day of joy and family closeness. It is a day when we put work aside and take time to relax. We can do that by going on a picnic, playing games, talking and laughing, or enjoying a special dinner together. It is also a good day to visit relatives or invite neighbors into our home. Just like the Risen Lord, Who spent Easter Sunday sharing peace and joy with His friends, we are meant to reach out and spread warmth and happiness to others. This is part of God's plan for our holiness.

Words to Know:

Holy Day of Obligation

Q. 43 *What does the Third Commandment, "Remember to keep holy the Lord's Day," tell us to do?*
The Third Commandment tells us to honor God on Sundays and Holy Days of Obligation by taking part in the Holy Mass (CCC 2180).

Q. 44 *What does the Third Commandment tell us not to do?*
The Third Commandment tells us not to miss Holy Mass on Sundays or do unnecessary work on Sundays and Holy Days of Obligation (CCC 2185).

11   Obedience and Love

"Lord, now let your servant depart in peace,
        according to your word. . . ."

Luke 2:29

We bring happiness to our home when we live up to God's Fourth Commandment: "Honor your father and your mother."

To **honor** means to love, respect, and obey. To **obey** means to do as we are told. God wants us to honor our parents because He brought us into the world through them. Once we were born, they gave us very much. Ever since we were tiny babies, our parents have loved, protected, and guided us. God entrusted us especially to them for that reason. They work and make sacrifices for us. They care for us every day. They give us all we need, whether it is a good meal to eat, new clothes as we grow, or surprises for our birthday.

Above all, they care for our souls. They want us to be good, so that we will be happy not only in this world but also for all eternity in Heaven. That is why they had us baptized and want us to receive the Sacraments and learn about our Faith.

When the Christ Child was growing up in Nazareth, He had many chances to love and obey His Mother and foster father, Joseph. Joseph was a carpenter and Jesus helped him carry the wood and hammer the nails. He surely also helped His Mother, Mary. We can picture Jesus doing these things kindly and cheerfully. Even though He was God, He respected His parents enough to obey and listen to them.

We discover the secret of the Holy Family's happiness every time we obey and offer to help. Some days it is hard to obey our parents because we would really rather play outside or go somewhere with our friends. When this happens, just remember that making sacrifices of

54

love makes us happiest of all in the end. Doing the right thing can be hard sometimes, but it will make us happy. Doing the wrong thing leaves a feeling of sadness inside us. This is part of our human nature because God made us to love Him, and we can only be happy when we obey the Commandments.

God wants us to respect and obey, not only our parents, but others who have lawful authority to protect us. For example, if we are at school and our teacher asks us to put away our artwork, listen without talking, or help a classmate who is in trouble we obey, and by doing so we please God.

In the Fourth Commandment God tells us to honor our father and mother, whom He gave us.

In the Fifth Commandment, God asks us to respect all human life. "You shall not kill," He tells us. The life of every person, no matter how poor, old, weak, or small, belongs to God and is precious. When you were inside your mother's womb and small enough to fit in the palm of a hand, God loved you and had a plan for your life. That is why the life of every baby inside of his mother is sacred and we respect it.

God wants us to respect the lives of people around us. In the Gospel, Jesus told the story of a man who was attacked by robbers when he was going down the road. They took his money and clothes and left him half dead. Three people passed the wounded man. The first two ignored him. The third one stopped to clean and bandage the man's wounds. Then he took the man to an inn and paid for his care and shelter. Jesus said that this Good Samaritan acted the way He wants us to act, especially toward the suffering and the poor. God will reward us if we show a readiness to make sacrifices for others and **good will**: always wanting to do what is right. He will bless us whenever we value, protect, or save the lives of others. Jesus said:

"Truly, I say to you, as you did it to one of the least of these my brethren, you did it to me" (Matthew 25:40).

On the other hand, it saddens God when we say mean things in anger, or refuse to make up with a friend after a fight. He wants us to be forgiving, loving, and generous. In our lifetime, He will give us many chances to be kind. We are kind when we help someone who is sick or disabled. We are kind when we hug a little brother or sister after he or she has fallen down. We are kind when we pray for people we do not like.

God wants us to respect our own lives, too. Our lives are a gift we must protect. When we try to eat the right foods to stay healthy or when we cross the street only when it is safe, we show God that we value His gift of life.

Words to Know:

honor   obey   good will

Q. 45 *What does the Fourth Commandment, "Honor your father and your mother," tell us to do?*
The Fourth Commandment tells us to love, respect, and obey our parents and our superiors (CCC 2197).

Q. 46 *What does the Fifth Commandment, "You shall not kill," tell us to do?*
The Fifth Commandment tells us to be of good will toward all, including our enemies, and to mend any bodily or spiritual wrong we do to our neighbor (CCC 2302–3).

Q. 47 *What does the Fifth Commandment tell us not to do?*
The Fifth Commandment tells us not to harm the life of anyone. This means that murder, suicide, fighting (out of anger), cursing, and giving scandal are wrong (CCC 2261–62).

"Even these may forget, yet I will not forget you. Behold, I have graven you on the palms of my hands."

Isaiah 49:15–16

58

12   Purity and Truth

"The commandments, 'You shall not commit adultery,
You shall not kill, You shall not steal, You shall not
covet,' and any other commandment, are summed up in
this sentence, 'You shall love your neighbor as yourself.'"

Romans 13:9

Have you ever thought about how important your body is? You speak with your body. You run, walk, and stand up to help someone with your body. With your five senses of touch, taste, sight, smell, and hearing, you are able to enjoy and learn about the world, and bring your talents to it.

God gave you your voice, your eyes, your hands, and all of your body for many wonderful reasons. Your body is holy because on the day of your Baptism, the Holy Spirit came to live inside of it. In the Sixth and Ninth Commandments, God told us to respect our bodies and the bodies of other people. He wants us to keep our bodies pure and pleasing to Him. We can have **purity** if we are clean in what we think, say, and do. He wants us to be modest and to stay away from movies, books, and pictures that are not good examples for us.

God also wants us to be faithful in our relationships with other people. For example, someday we may marry a person we love. God will expect us to be faithful to the love and promises we vow on our wedding day. If we strive to keep our vows, God will help us and reward us richly.

The Seventh Commandment and the Tenth Commandment tell us to be fair with property. God wants us to be satisfied with what we have, not to covet what others have. To **covet** is to want wrongfully something that does not belong to you. We are also to respect other people's things. God told us, "You shall not steal." If someone takes a snack or a toy or money that belongs to someone else, he is breaking God's Law. Cheating on tests, borrowing things and not returning them, or being dishonest in a store breaks the same Law.

We can obey the Seventh and Tenth Commandments by being satisfied with the things we have, by taking care of them, and by sharing them. It pleases God when we give or share a snack, a toy, or money that belongs to us.

God also wants us to take special care of other people's things. If we borrow a book from the library, we should take good care of it and return it on time. If we accidentally break something that belongs to someone else, God wants us to make up for it, either by paying for it or replacing it. This is called justice or fairness.

If four children are playing ball on the front lawn and by mistake their ball smashes a neighbor's window, they have some choices. They can run away and pretend it did not happen. They can lie and say that someone else broke the window. They can keep playing ball and not worry about it. Or they can go to the neighbor, tell him what really happened, then help pay for the damage. Which choice do you think obeys the Seventh and Tenth Commandments?

The Eighth Commandment tells us to be honest: "You shall not **bear false witness** against your neighbor" (tell a lie). This means that we should always speak the truth. The **truth** means how things really are. God loves the truth. When Jesus was on earth He spoke the truth in all things, even when it did not make Him popular. He wants us to do the same.

Sometimes we are afraid to tell the truth or we want to blame someone else for something we did. But God asks that we be honest with ourselves and others. **Honesty** means telling the truth. If we are honest and keep our promises, we will be like Jesus Who is the Truth.

"Blessed are the pure in heart, for they shall see God."

Matthew 5:8

Many holy people have even died for the truth. Saint Thomas More is one example. He was a special friend and helper of King Henry the Eighth in England during the sixteenth century. One day the king decided to disobey God and make himself head of the Church. He asked Thomas More to agree with him. But Thomas refused because this was not right. The king's judges tried to force Thomas to lie. When they could not succeed, they put him to death. Thomas told the English people, "I die the king's good servant, but God's first." Thomas More had integrity, which means he was true to himself and to God. His honesty helped him get to Heaven.

Can you think of any other saints or holy people who have suffered to witness to the truth?

Words to Know:

purity   covet   bear false witness
          truth   honesty

Q. 48   *What does the Eighth Commandment, "You shall not lie," tell us to do?*
The Eighth Commandment tells us to speak the truth carefully and to think the best of our neighbor (CCC 2469, 2478).

Q. 49 *What does the Eighth Commandment tell us not to do?*
The Eighth Commandment tells us not to harm another person's reputation. This includes false witness, lies, flattery, unfounded suspicion, and rash judgment (CCC 2477–78).

Q. 50 *What must a person do, who has damaged his neighbor's good name by falsely accusing him or speaking wickedly of him?*
He who has damaged his neighbor's good name by false accusation or wicked talk, must repair the damage he has done, so far as he is able (CCC 2487).

Q. 51 *What does the Sixth Commandment, "You shall not commit adultery," tell us not to do?*
The Sixth Commandment tells us not to be impure. This means that it is wrong to use immoral words or view books, pictures, and shows that are bad examples for us (CCC 2339).

Q. 52 *What does the Ninth Commandment, "You shall not covet your neighbor's wife," tell us not to do?*
The Ninth Commandment tells us not to have impure thoughts and desires (CCC 2514–15).

Q. 53 *What does the Seventh Commandment, "You shall not steal," tell us to do?*
The Seventh Commandment tells us to give back property belonging to others, to fix

damages that we cause, and to pay our debts
(CCC 2412, 2454).

Q. 54 *What does the Seventh Commandment tell us
not to do?*
The Seventh Commandment tells us not to
damage our neighbor's property. This includes
theft and damaging actions. It is wrong to help
those who do such damages (CCC 2401).

Q. 55 *If we have stolen or damaged our neighbor's
property, should we try to make restitution?*
Yes, if we have stolen or damaged our
neighbor's property, we should try to make
restitution (CCC 2412).

Q. 56 *What does the Tenth Commandment, "You shall
not covet your neighbor's goods," tell us to do?*
The Tenth Commandment tells us to be just in
the desire to improve our lives, and to suffer
with patience the hardships and other sufferings
permitted by the Lord for our own good (CCC
2544).

Q. 57 *What does the Tenth Commandment tell us
not to do?*
The Tenth Commandment tells us not to have an
unhealthy desire for riches, which would make
us forget the rights and welfare of our neighbors
(CCC 2534, 2536).

13   God's Tender Mercy

"My enemies say of me in malice:
    'When will he die, and his name perish?'"

Psalms 41:5

Jesus told many stories to show us how deep God's love is. God's love follows us wherever we go. Even when we commit sins, God does not stop loving us. He waits and watches for us to return. The moment we say we are sorry, He welcomes us back with open arms. No sin on earth will ever be greater than His mercy and love.

Jesus told the story about a shepherd who loved his sheep. The shepherd gave his flock fresh water and food. He protected it from wolves. He knew all of His lambs by name and was willing to lay down His life for them to protect them from danger. One day a lamb got lost and the shepherd did not rest until he found it. When the lamb came back, the shepherd said, "Rejoice with me, because I have found my lost sheep." Then Jesus told us He was the Good Shepherd and we were His sheep. He compared the story to His love for us: "In the same way, there is great joy in Heaven whenever anyone is sorry for his sins."

Jesus did more than tell stories about **forgiveness**. He forgave many sinners. Some of the sinners were among His own friends. Peter the Apostle denied Jesus three times on the night He was betrayed. After Peter realized what he had done and wept with sorrow, Jesus forgave him completely.

Jesus' love and mercy gave hope to people with very bad sins. It invited them to be good. Mary Magdalene was a great sinner, but she believed in Jesus and the Good News of God's love. One night she came up to Jesus, poured precious oil on His feet, and wept for forgiveness. That was all Mary had to do. Jesus told everyone, "This woman's sins are forgiven because she has loved much."

Only God can forgive sins. But on the first Easter Sunday night, Jesus gave His Apostles the power to forgive sins in His name. This was a great gift of grace to the world. Jesus breathed on the Apostles and said, "Peace be with you. Receive the Holy Spirit; if you forgive men's sins, they are forgiven."

The Apostles were the early priests of the Church. Our priests today carry the same power to forgive sins. They do this through the Sacrament of Penance. This Sacrament frees our souls of any **mortal sins**, which are very serious and remove God's life of **grace** from our souls. It also frees us of less serious, **venial sins** that make a soul weak and less pleasing to God. When we go to a priest for this Sacrament, we can be sure that Christ Himself is present, and He washes away all our sins. He will never turn us away when we are truly sorry for our sins, but He will only hold us closer to His Heart.

Remember, Jesus was crucified on a Cross between two thieves. The thief on Jesus' left had no sorrow for his crimes. But the thief on Jesus' right cried out that he was sorry. Jesus forgave him and said to him, "Today you will be with me in Paradise" (Luke 23:43).

Words to Know:

forgiveness   mortal sin   grace   venial sin

Q. 58 *In how many ways is sin committed?*
Sin is committed in four ways, in *thoughts*, in *words*, in *deeds*, and in *omissions*, things we fail to do (CCC 1849).

Q. 59 *How many kinds of sin are there?*
Sin is of two kinds: *mortal* and *venial* (CCC 1854).

Q. 60 *What is mortal sin?*
Mortal sin is a serious wrong done on purpose with full knowledge that it is wrong (CCC 1857).

Q. 61 *What is venial sin?*
Venial sin is a less serious wrong, or a serious wrong that is done without full knowledge of its seriousness or full consent (CCC 1862).

Q. 62 *Are all sins equal?*
No, sins are not all equal. Just as some venial sins are less light than others, some mortal sins are more serious and harmful than others (CCC 1854).

Q. 63 *What is Confession?*
Confession is the Sacrament instituted by Jesus Christ to forgive the sins committed after Baptism. Confession is also called the Sacrament of Penance or Reconciliation (CCC 1446).

Q. 64 *When was the Sacrament of Confession instituted by Jesus Christ?*
The Sacrament of Confession was instituted by Jesus Christ when He said to the Apostles, "Receive the Holy Spirit. If you forgive the sins of any, they are forgiven; if you retain the sins of any, they are retained" (John 20:22–23, CCC 1441).

14 Meeting Jesus In Confession

"If you forgive the sins of any, they are forgiven; if you retain the sins of any, they are retained."

John 20:23

If you know you have hurt someone you love, what should you do? The best thing to do is to go to that person and say you are sorry. It is not enough just to think about how sorry you are. A good friendship calls for more. A true friend will go to the person he has hurt, say he is sorry, and make up and be friends again.

In the **Sacrament of Penance**, that is what we do with Jesus. We go to Him, tell Him we are sorry, resolve not to sin again, accept His forgiveness, and keep our friendship with Him alive and strong.

To prepare ourselves for this Sacrament, there are certain things we must do. First we ask God the Holy Spirit, Who lives inside us, to help us remember our sins. We think about what we have done wrong and how many times we have done it. This is called **examination of conscience**.

Next, we think about how our sins offend Jesus and how we are sorry for them. This is called **sorrow for sins**. We make up our minds not to commit the same sins again, and we say an Act of Contrition. **Contrition** means sorrow. An Act of Contrition is a prayer telling God we are sorry and we hate our sins. In the Act of Contrition we say we hate sin because we know it can keep us from Heaven, but much more importantly, because it offends God. We tell God that He is all good and deserving of all our love. We ask for His grace to do better in the future.

After our Act of Contrition, it is time to receive the Sacrament. We go into the confessional or reconciliation room where the priest welcomes us. Together we make the Sign of the Cross. The priest may read to us from the Bible. Usually he says words about God's mercy and love.

We tell the priest how long it has been since our last Confession, then we confess our sins since that time. After we are all finished, the priest talks to us about what we have told him. Then he gives us a **penance**, which can be some prayers or action that helps to make up for the wrong we have done to God and to others. (We will do the penance after our Confession is over.) Then we say the Act of Contrition out loud.

Before we leave the confessional, the priest will absolve us. This means that he uses his Christ-given power to forgive all our sins. When we hear the words of absolution, we know that Jesus Himself is forgiving us through the priest. He says, "I absolve you from your sins in the Name of the Father, and of the Son, and of the Holy Spirit." We accept the absolution by answering, "Amen." This is a beautiful moment, because God has completely forgiven us. He is giving us a fresh start.

Every time we receive the Sacrament of Penance, Jesus is with us, healing our hearts. We always confess our sins privately to a priest, usually in the confessional. Sometimes, at a communal Penance service, all the people in the church prepare together for Confession and then confess and receive absolution individually. In cases of necessity, where to hear individual Confessions of large numbers of people is impossible, a priest may give general absolution to all the people. But those people then have to make a private, individual Confession as soon as they are able.

Jesus waits for us in this Sacrament because He has so much merciful love and grace to give us. Let us try to go to Him often.

ACT OF CONTRITION

O my God, I am heartily sorry for having offended You. I detest all my sins because of Your just punishments, but most of all because they offend You, my God, Who are all good and deserving of all my love. I firmly resolve, with the help of Your grace, to confess my sins, to do penance, and to amend my life. *Amen.*

THE WORDS OF ABSOLUTION

God, the Father of mercies, through the death and Resurrection of His Son, has reconciled the world to Himself and sent the Holy Spirit among us for the forgiveness of sins; through the ministry of the Church, may God give you pardon and peace, and I absolve you from your sins in the Name of the Father, and of the Son, and of the Holy Spirit.

Words to Know:

Sacrament of Penance   examination of conscience
sorrow for sins   contrition   penance

Q. 65 *How many things are required to make a good Confession?*
To make a good Confession five things are required: 1) examination of conscience; 2) sorrow for sins; 3) the intention of not committing sin again; 4) the accusation of our sin; 5) satisfaction or penance (CCC 1450, 1454, 1456, 1459).

Q. 66 *How is the examination of conscience done?*
The examination of conscience is done by remembering the sins we have committed in thoughts, words, deeds, and omissions against the Commandments of God, beginning from our last good Confession (CCC 1454).

Q. 67 *What is sorrow?*
Sorrow is a sadness and hatred for the sins we have committed, which makes us decide not to sin again (CCC 1451).

15   The Christ Child Is Born

"Behold, a virgin shall conceive and bear a son,
and his name shall be called Emmanuel. . . ."

Matthew 1:23

How would you feel if you and your family sat for a long time in a
cold, dark room with no light? That is how the people of Israel might
sometimes have felt during their long wait for the Messiah. They
waited in darkness for two thousand years. At last God kept His
promise. He sent the world a Savior Who shattered the darkness with
a great light. Jesus is the Light of the World.

God did not send a rich king or strong warrior to be the Light of
the World. He sent a little child. This child was His own Son, the
Second Person of the Blessed Trinity. Jesus is God, but He was born
into the world as a man like us. God the Father invited Mary to be a
part of this special plan to save His people. Jesus came to the world
because Mary answered yes.

Mary was a young woman of Nazareth. She was in her simple,
village home one day when the angel Gabriel appeared before her to
bring God's message:

"Hail, full of grace, the Lord is with you....You will
conceive in your womb and bear a son, and you shall call
his name Jesus....The Holy Spirit will come upon you,
and the power of the Most High will overshadow you;
therefore the child to be born will be called holy, the Son
of God" (Luke 1:28, 31, 35).

73

74

Mary knew if she said yes it might mean great sorrows as well as great joys. But she wanted to do whatever God asked. She bowed her head and told the angel: "Behold, I am the handmaid of the Lord, let it be to me according to your word." Mary's quiet yes was still a secret to God's people, but it was the beginning of His loving plan to save them from sin.

An ordinary girl might have been afraid. But Mary was special. God prepared her to be the Mother of the Savior even before she was born. He had given her a gift which we call Mary's Immaculate Conception. This means that Mary was created free from Original Sin. From the moment she was conceived in her mother's womb, her soul was filled with sanctifying grace. Mary did not need to be baptized because she always had God's life in her soul. This is why she was worthy to be the Mother of Jesus. God also chose a good man named Joseph to marry her and be the foster father of Jesus. A **foster father** is a man who takes the place of the real father.

On the night of Jesus' birth, Mary and Joseph walked from inn to inn looking for shelter. They were in the town of **Bethlehem** because the Roman governor made all people return to their hometowns. The little town of Bethlehem was full. Every innkeeper told Joseph, "Sorry, there is no room for you in this inn."

At last, Joseph found a **stable** under the stars. Animals were sheltered beneath its roof. Jesus was born that night among the gentle oxen, donkeys, and lambs. Mary wrapped Him tenderly in soft cloth and laid Him in a **manger**, a box that held food for the animals. The Son of God spent His first earthly hours on a **humble** bed of straw.

An angel appeared to shepherds on the hillsides near Bethlehem and proclaimed, "Behold, I bring you Good News of great joy! Today, in the town of David, has been born to you a Savior, Who is Christ the Lord. You will find Him lying in a manger." Full of wonder, the shepherds ran to be the first to adore Him. Later three wise men followed a great star to find the Child. They brought Him precious gifts for a King: gold, frankincense, and myrrh. We can bring the Christ Child our hearts, as our gifts for Him.

Christmas is Jesus' birthday. Every year we sing carols to celebrate. This carol was written over a hundred years ago:

WE THREE KINGS OF ORIENT ARE

We three kings of Orient are,
Bearing gifts we traverse afar,
Field and fountain, Moor and mountain,
Following yonder star.

O star of wonder star of night,
Star with royal beauty bright;
Westward leading, still proceeding,
Guide us to thy perfect light.

Born a King on Bethlehem's plain,
Gold I bring to crown Him again,
King for ever, ceasing never
Over us all to reign.

Words to Know:

foster father   Bethlehem   stable   manger   humble

"Glory to God in the highest, and on earth peace among men with whom he is well pleased!"

Luke 2:14

Q. 68   *Did Jesus Christ always exist?*
As God, Jesus Christ has always existed; as man, He began to exist from the moment of the Incarnation (CCC 461, 470).

Q. 69   *From whom was Jesus Christ born?*
Jesus Christ was born of Mary ever-virgin, who therefore is the Mother of God (CCC 485, 495–96, 499).

Q. 70   *Was Saint Joseph the father of Jesus Christ?*
Saint Joseph was not the *true* father of Jesus Christ; as the spouse of Mary and the guardian of Jesus, he was the foster father of Jesus (CCC 532).

Q. 71   *Where was Jesus Christ born?*
Jesus Christ was born at Bethlehem, in a stable, and He was placed in a manger (CCC 525).

Q. 72   *Why did Jesus Christ wish to be poor?*
Jesus Christ wished to be poor in order to teach us to be humble and not to place our happiness in the riches and the pleasures of this world (CCC 526).

Q. 73   *What is the Epiphany?*
The Epiphany is a feast celebrated to remember how the wise men followed a star to Bethlehem to adore Jesus, bringing Him gifts fit for a king. This event shows that Jesus is Savior of the whole world (CCC 528).

16   Jesus Grows in Age and Wisdom

"And Jesus increased in wisdom and in stature, and in favor with God and man."

Luke 2:52

As a boy growing up in Nazareth, Jesus led an ordinary life. He ate, slept, laughed, played, worked, and studied. Even though He was God, He was truly human and He grew up and learned things just as we do. Since Jesus was Jewish, He learned all the Jewish customs and traditions of His time.

Joseph, a skilled carpenter, probably taught Jesus how to make fine things from wood. As a tiny boy, Jesus could only watch and pick up the wood chips as they fell. The neighbors of the Holy Family must have loved Jesus very much, but they had no idea that He was God's own Son. Only Mary and Joseph knew that. It was still hidden from the rest of the world. That is why we call the first thirty years of Jesus' time on earth His "hidden life."

Even though Jesus was living a "hidden" life, none of it was hidden from God the Father. God watched every moment of it. God sees every moment of *our* hidden lives too. He sees all the times we sacrifice something we would rather do to obey our parents. For example, you might want to play with a friend, but your mother needs you to set the table. Or you might want to finish a book, but your father needs you to help him rake the lawn. When we offer up our little disappointments or boredom and obey our parents with love, God sees it all. He blesses us for acting as Jesus did when He was growing up.

When the time came, Jesus left His quiet life in Nazareth. He put away the tools of a carpenter and started working to fulfill God's plan of salvation.

God sent a prophet to prepare the way for Jesus. This prophet told people in a loud, clear voice, "Get ready! The Promised One is coming! Be sorry for your sins." This holy man was named **John the Baptist**. He baptized with a baptism of repentance all the people who listened and were sorry for their sins.

One day Jesus Himself came to John to be baptized in the waters of the Jordan River. As Jesus came out of the water, God gave a wonderful sign. The Holy Spirit came down upon Him in the form of a dove, and the voice of His Father called from Heaven: "This is My Beloved Son with Whom I am well pleased." Now Jesus was ready to begin His public life in His mission as the Savior of the world.

At your own Baptism, the Holy Spirit came upon you, too. He came inside your soul and filled it with God's life of grace. On that happy day, God silently told you, "You are My beloved child, and I love you." Just as with Jesus, our Baptism has prepared us for a mission. Our mission on earth is to love God with all our hearts and to love each other.

Words to Know:

John the Baptist

Q. 74 *Who is John the Baptist?*
John the Baptist is the last of the prophets. He prepared the way for Jesus and baptized Him in the Jordan River (CCC 523).

Q. 75 *What special event happened at Jesus' Baptism in the Jordan?*
When Jesus was baptized in the Jordan, the Holy Spirit came down upon Him in the form of a dove and God the Father spoke from Heaven, saying, "This is My Beloved Son, in Whom I am well pleased (CCC 535).

Q. 76 *How is your Baptism like the Baptism of Jesus?*
At my Baptism, the Holy Spirit came upon me to bring God's Life of grace into my soul and to prepare me for the work God has planned for me to do (CCC 1265, 1268, 1270).

82

17   Signs and Wonders

"When the people saw the sign which he had done, they said, 'This is indeed the prophet who is to come into the world!'"

John 6:14

When He was about thirty years old, Jesus the Savior began making His presence clear to the People of God. He started preaching the Good News of the Kingdom of God in the area called Galilee. Crowds came from all over to hear Him speak. They were fascinated because Jesus was telling them things they had never heard before. He told them, "I am the Way, the Truth, and the Life."

Jesus performed many miracles to prove He was the Savior and the Son of God. A **miracle** is something wonderful that is done by the power of God. It is something only God can do. Once a bride and groom in Cana ran out of wine at their wedding feast. Jesus solved their problem by changing the water in six stone jars into good wine.

Another time, Jesus fed a crowd of five thousand on five loaves of bread and two fish! People had crowded the hillsides all day to hear Him preach, and Jesus knew they were hungry. The Apostles warned Him there was not enough food. Jesus blessed the handful of loaves and fishes and suddenly there was enough food for everyone. All five thousand people were amazed to get a delicious dinner in the hills that day.

Most of the time, Jesus performed miracles to heal the suffering. At His word or touch, the blind could see, the lame walked, and the sick got well. All of this gave people great faith in Jesus.

Once a Roman soldier trusted in Jesus' power so much that he asked Jesus to heal his sick servant. When Jesus said, "I will go to heal him," the soldier said, "Lord, I am not worthy that You should come under my roof. Only say the word, and I know my servant will be healed." Jesus marveled at this man's trust and belief. He said, "Go your way. Because you have believed, your servant is cured." Later the Roman soldier learned that his servant had been cured at that very instant.

The Roman centurion's trust in Jesus' power to heal is remembered every time we go to Holy Mass. Right before Holy Communion we tell Jesus, "Lord, I am not worthy that you should enter under my roof, but only say the word and my soul shall be healed."

Jesus' power to perform miracles was even stronger than death. He brought back to life a man named Lazarus who had been buried for four days. All hope seemed lost, but Jesus promised Lazarus' good sisters, "Your brother will rise." Then He ordered the stone to be rolled back from the tomb, and He called to Lazarus. Lazarus arose, alive and well, and all the people rejoiced in amazement.

Jesus came to heal people's souls. He taught them to love God the Father, to stop sinning, and to be holy. He gave them **parables**, or stories, that explained the Kingdom of God. One parable was about a mustard seed. A mustard seed is very tiny, but when planted in the ground it grows to be a huge tree. Jesus compared the mustard seed to His own Kingdom. It had small beginnings, but would cover the whole world.

He told another parable about a farmer sowing seeds. Some of the seeds fell on good ground and they yielded a rich harvest. Other seeds fell on rocks and thorns and they yielded nothing. Jesus said the seeds were like the Word of God falling on the ears of good men and bad men. If it falls on the good soil of a faithful heart, it yields many good things. If it falls on the poor soil of a stubborn heart, it can yield nothing at all.

Jesus found both friends and enemies on earth. His friends were the Apostles and disciples who followed Him. His enemies were the ones who doubted and made fun of Him. These enemies could not understand a Savior Who ate with sinners and Who loved the poor. Many of the Jewish leaders, such as the Pharisees, were jealous of Jesus. They hated Him because He pointed out their faults. They were too proud to follow Jesus' teachings of love because it would mean changing their lives. They did not have the courage to become humble, forgiving, and loving like Jesus.

Words to Know:

miracle   parable

Q. 77 *What is the mystery of the Son of God made man called?*
The mystery of the Son of God made man is called the Incarnation (CCC 461).

Q. 78 *Who is Jesus Christ?*
Jesus Christ is the Second Person of the Blessed Trinity, the Son of God made man (CCC 470).

Q. 79 *Is Jesus Christ God and man?*
Yes, Jesus Christ is true God and true man (CCC 470).

Q. 80 *Why did Jesus work miracles?*
Jesus worked miracles to show that He is God and the Kingdom is present in Him. His miracles were to gather people into the Kingdom of God (CCC 542, 547).

Q. 81 *Why did Jesus tell parables?*
Jesus told parables to teach people about the Kingdom of God and invite them into it (CCC 546).

18   The Last Supper, Our First Mass

"This is my body which is for you. Do this in remembrance of me."

1 Corinthians 11:24

The night before Jesus died, He and the Apostles gathered to celebrate the feast of Passover. This Jewish feast was a holy dinner held once a year. It honored the sacred memory of the time when God saved Moses and His Chosen People from slavery in Egypt.

On the Passover night that Jesus and His Apostles gathered, God was about to save His people again. This time He would save them from the darkness of sin and death. He would unlock the gates of Heaven and make it possible for them to live with Him in joy for ever.

Jesus, our Savior, was about to pay a great price to win this grace. He was about to lay down His own life so that we could go to Heaven. Jesus knew His death was very near. Sitting at the Passover table that night, Jesus felt tender sadness at the thought of leaving His friends. He wanted them to be strong and holy when He was gone.

"Little children, yet a little while I am with you. . . .
A new commandment I give to you, that you love one another; even as I have loved you, that you also love one another. By this all men will know that you are my disciples, if you have love for one another."

John 13:33–35

88

First Jesus gave them a lesson in holiness. He knelt down to wash their feet. Peter told Him, "Master, You will never wash my feet." However, Jesus told Peter that friends love and serve one another without shame. He told the twelve Apostles, "If I, the Lord and Master, have washed your feet, you also ought to wash the feet of one another. For I have given you an example; that as I have done to you, so you also should do."

Later, while they were eating, a very important moment came. Jesus took bread, blessed and broke it, and gave it to His disciples saying, "This is my Body, which will be given up for you."

Then He took a cup of wine. He gave thanks and gave it to them saying, "This is the chalice of my Blood, the Blood of the new and eternal covenant, which will be poured out for you and for many for the forgiveness of sins."

When Jesus spoke those words, the bread and wine were changed into His Body and Blood. It still looked and tasted like ordinary food, but it was Jesus. When the Apostles ate it, Jesus came into their souls. They were the first ones ever to receive Holy Communion.

Jesus told the Apostles, "Do this in **remembrance** of Me." With these words, Jesus gave the Apostles the power to change bread and wine into the Body and Blood of Jesus Christ.

The **Last Supper** was actually the first Mass. It took place on a Thursday, the night before Jesus died. Every year on **Holy Thursday** we especially remember the first Mass and Jesus' gift of the Holy Eucharist and of the priesthood.

Holy Communion was not meant just for the Apostles. It was meant for all of Jesus' followers until the end of time. At every Holy Mass the priest says the same words over bread and wine, and they become the Body and Blood of Jesus. We call this the Sacrament of the Holy Eucharist. Whenever we receive it, Jesus comes into our hearts, alive and full of love.

Words to Know:

remembrance   Last Supper   Holy Thursday

"I am the bread of life; he who comes to me shall not hunger, and he who believes in me shall never thirst."

John 6:35

Q. 82   *When was the first Mass celebrated?*
Jesus celebrated the first Mass with his Apostles on Holy Thursday, the night before he died (CCC 1340).

Q. 83 *What is the Sacrament of the Holy Eucharist?*
The Holy Eucharist is the Sacrament in which Jesus is present under the appearance of bread and wine (CCC 1337, 1374).

Q. 84 *What does the priest say over the bread and wine?*
The priest says the same words Jesus said at the Last Supper. Over the bread he says, "This is my Body, which will be given up for you." Over the wine he says, "This is the chalice of my Blood, the Blood of the new and eternal covenant, which will be poured out for you and for many for the forgiveness of sins" (CCC 1333, 1339, 1375).

Q. 85 *What happens to the bread and wine when the priest says the words of Jesus?*
When the priest says the words of Jesus over the bread and wine, by the power of the Holy Spirit, the bread and wine change entirely into the Body, Blood, Soul, and Divinity of Jesus. The appearances of bread and wine remain, but Jesus is truly present (CCC 1374–75).

Q. 86 *What is Holy Communion?*
Holy Communion is the way we unite ourselves to Jesus by receiving Him into ourselves. He comes into us and gives us His life and grace. By Holy Communion, Jesus makes us sharers in His Body and Blood to form one single Body in Christ (CCC 1331).

92

19 Jesus Gives His Life for Us

"Greater love has no man than this, that a man lay down his life for his friends."

John 15:13

After the Last Supper, Jesus went out to pray in the Garden of Olives. He asked His disciples to stay awake with Him for a little while, but they fell asleep. Jesus was alone in His great suffering.

Jesus saw all of our sins that night and it saddened Him. He thought of all the suffering He would accept to make up for our sins. Remember, Jesus was both God and man. As a man, He felt deep emotions. That night He felt sadness and fear. He asked God the Father, "If it is possible, take this suffering away from Me." But then He told Him, "Your will, not Mine, be done." God the Father sent an angel to comfort Him.

Later in the night, soldiers came to arrest Jesus. These soldiers were cruel, but Jesus was gentle and went with them. He knew He was about to fulfill His Father's plan for our salvation. Jesus bravely went before the high priest and Jewish leaders. He was silent when they wrongly accused Him and wanted Him to be put to death.

By law, the Jewish leaders could not put Jesus to death. They needed Pontius Pilate, the Roman governor of Judea, to condemn Him. Pilate also had the power to set Jesus free. He knew Jesus was innocent. But Pilate was too afraid of not being popular. When an angry crowd kept yelling out, "Crucify Him!" Pilate gave in. He did not protect Jesus. He sentenced Him to death as His enemies wanted.

The soldiers grabbed Jesus and treated Him like a criminal. They beat Him with whips. They pushed a crown of sharp thorns on His head. They made fun of Him by saying in disrespectful voices, "Hail, King of the Jews."

Now Jesus was very weak, but the soldiers hurt Him even more. They made Him carry a heavy Cross. They gave Him no rest or water. Jesus fell down three times, but they made Him go on. When Jesus reached the top of Mount **Calvary**, they nailed His hands and feet to the wood of the Cross, raised the Cross upright, and left Him to die in pain.

Even in the midst of great suffering, Jesus was full of love. He asked His Father to forgive the cruel soldiers. He gave hope and forgiveness to a thief hanging by His side. He told His Mother Mary to be the Mother of His beloved Apostle John, and of the whole world.

Some of the people laughed at Jesus and said, "He heals others, but He cannot save Himself!" Jesus was God, and He had full power to escape the pain of the Cross. But He stayed on the Cross. He freely chose to suffer and die because He loved us so much. He wanted to make up for our sins. He wanted to **redeem** us, or buy our freedom, so we could go to Heaven.

A **sacrifice** is something that is offered to God. Jesus' sacrifice was so complete and so perfect that it conquered death for ever. It healed the wounds of Adam's Original Sin. It restored full friendship between man and God.

Jesus' great victory taught us the value of sacrifice. His **Passion** and death saved the world. When we offer up things out of love, we are part of Jesus' great sacrifice. We make up for our sins and the sins of others. In some way we help Him in saving the world. Small acts of self-denial can be as simple as giving up a piece of candy we want

94

to keep or helping our mother when we are tired. These acts of love become part of Jesus' sacrifice and help bring grace into the world.

The next time you go to Mass, find the Stations of the Cross in your church. Look at all fourteen images. Remember that Jesus loved you so much He suffered and died for you. You must be very precious to Him. Tell Him that you will love Him forever.

STATIONS OF THE CROSS

1. Jesus is condemned to death.
2. Jesus carries His Cross.
3. Jesus falls the first time.
4. Jesus meets His Mother.
5. Jesus is helped by Simon.
6. Veronica wipes the face of Jesus.
7. Jesus falls a second time.
8. Jesus speaks to the women.
9. Jesus falls a third time.
10. Jesus is stripped of His clothes.
11. Jesus is nailed to the Cross.
12. Jesus dies on the Cross.
13. Jesus is taken down from the Cross.
14. Jesus is placed in the tomb.

Words to Know:

Calvary   redeem   sacrifice   Passion

Q. 87 *Why did the Son of God become man?*
The Son of God became man to save us, that is, to redeem us from sin and to regain Heaven for us (CCC 461).

Q. 88 *What did Jesus Christ do to save us?*
To save us, Jesus Christ paid for our sins by suffering and sacrificing Himself on the Cross, and He taught us how to live according to God (CCC 571, 580).

Q. 89 *What is a sacrifice?*
Sacrifice is the public offering to God of something to show that God is the Creator and Supreme Master to Whom everything belongs (CCC 606).

Q. 90 *What are the Stations of the Cross?*
The Stations of the Cross are a devotional prayer in which we think about the suffering and death of Jesus (CCC 1674, 1676).

"Let not your hearts be troubled. . . . And when I go and prepare a place for you, I will come again and will take you to myself, that where I am you may be also."

John 14:1–3

20   Offering Gifts of Love

"This chalice which is poured out for you is the new
covenant in my blood."

Luke 22:20

All through the ages, God's children have offered sacrifices to Him
as a sign of their worship and love. During the Old Testament days,
before Jesus came to earth, the People of God offered up many things
that were dear to them. In this way they told God that they loved His
gifts, but they loved Him even more.

Whenever a person offered up something in sacrifice, he burned or
destroyed it. This showed that he was giving it completely back to
God. Farmers thanked God for their crops by sacrificing the first
fruits of their harvest. It was a way of saying, "We believe that these
gifts are from You. Thank You. Please keep blessing us."

So men made a present to the Heavenly Father of the very things
that nourished them and kept them alive. Healthful grains like barley,
wheat, and oats were baked into unleavened bread and cakes. Grapes
were pressed into wine. Then the good grain and wine were given to
God as gifts.

People of the Old Testament also offered up the bloody sacrifice of
animals. They used cows, sheep, and doves. During an animal
sacrifice, the priest placed the victim on an altar and put his hands on
it. Then he killed the animal, shed its blood, and burned it.

Holy men of the Old Testament were generous in these sacrifices.
Abel, who was a shepherd, offered up his best lamb. The first thing
Noah did after the flood was build a stone altar and sacrifice some
animals from the ark. Abraham was even willing to obey God's
request that he sacrifice his own beloved son, Isaac. God was only

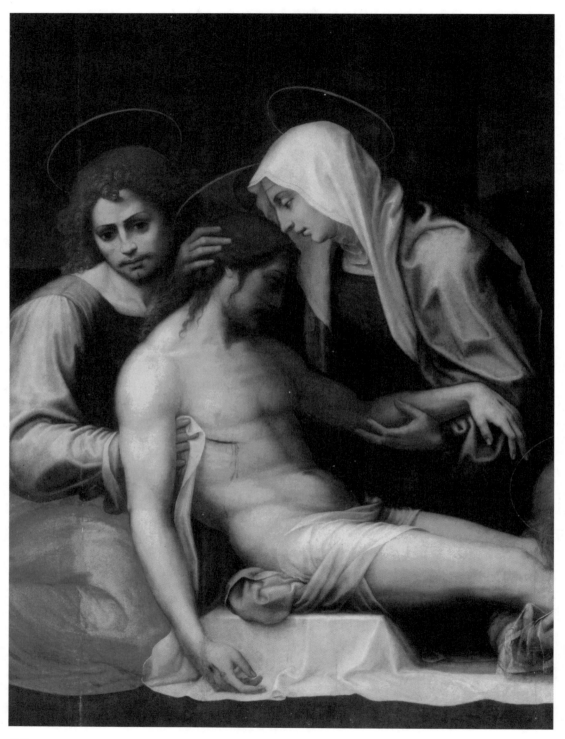

testing Abraham's trust and love. He rewarded Abraham by stopping him and showing him a ram he could sacrifice instead.

In time, God had Moses anoint a few men to offer up gifts for all the people. These men were called priests. The people joined the priests in praying to God. Some of these prayers were cries for help or sorrow for sin. Others were gifts of praise or thanks.

Every Old Testament sacrifice had one great goal in common. Man deeply longed to make up for sin. Man wanted to restore his friendship with God.

When Jesus came into the world, people were still trying to restore friendship with God. Jewish families went to worship God at the **Temple** in Jerusalem. They offered up lambs, doves, and food. God was pleased with these sacrifices. But He wanted to give His people a far greater gift to offer. He wanted to give them one gift that would unite them with Him to the end of time. And He wanted to give them a perfect gift.

Jesus, God's beloved Son, was that perfect gift. When He shed His Blood and died on the Cross, He gave God that perfect gift as a sacrifice on our behalf. The sacrifice of Himself was so perfect and true that it was the best gift ever given to God. It was so powerful that it washed away Adam's sin and all sin and so saved the whole human race. It opened the Father's heart and the gates of Heaven.

Jesus knew that men and women in all of history would want and need to share in this perfect gift to God, too. So He made it possible for the perfect gift of His Body and Blood to be offered continually. On the night before He died, Jesus gave His Apostles the power to change bread and wine into His Body and Blood in the Sacrifice of the **Mass**.

Today all over the world the Sacrifice of the Mass continues in the same way. Listen to the words of the priest. "Take this, all of you, and eat of it, for this is my Body. . . . Take this, all of you, and drink from it, for this is the chalice of my Blood. . . ." Every time we go to Holy Mass, we offer up Christ Himself to the Father. It is the very same sacrifice as the one on Calvary.

On the Cross Jesus offered Himself, shedding His Blood for our redemption. Through the ministry of the priest Jesus is offered on the altar again without shedding His Blood. At Mass we not only remember Jesus' sacrifice of Himself to the Father, we continue it. Each time, Jesus brings His sacrifice before us in a real but sacramental way. He is the Lamb of God being offered continually to save our world. We can share in this perfect gift to God at each Mass. Together with the priest we offer Jesus to the Father. This is the most pleasing and powerful gift we can ever give God. It is our most wonderful offering. It unites us with God and fills our world with His life and love.

Words to Know:

Temple   Mass

Q. 91   *What is the Holy Mass?*
The Holy Mass is the sacrifice of the Body and Blood of Jesus Christ. The Holy Mass is offered on the altar by the priest of God, under the appearances of bread and wine, in memory of the Sacrifice of the Cross (CCC 1364–65).

Q. 92   *Is the Sacrifice of the Mass the same sacrifice as the Sacrifice of the Cross?*
The Sacrifice of the Mass is the Sacrifice of the Cross; the only difference is in the manner of performing it (CCC 1366–67).

21   The Holy Mass

"Then they told what had happened on the road, and
how he was known to them in the breaking of the
bread."

Luke 24:35

Jesus' sacrifice on the Cross healed a great wound. It reunited
man and God in full friendship for the first time since the
disobedience of Adam and Eve. This Sacrifice paid the price of
our sins. It opened the gates of Heaven. It was the most perfect
gift a man ever gave to God. Jesus became a man for this very
purpose. The gift of His life was so powerful that He wants us to
continue offering it to the Father until the end of time.

At the Last Supper, Jesus gave us a way to do that. He passed on
to the Apostles, and through them to all priests, His power to bless
and change the bread and wine. Now at every Mass this miracle
happens. Through the priest the bread and wine become Christ's own
Body and Blood. Then the priest lifts up the Sacred Host and Cup of
salvation and offers them to the Father. Christ, the Lamb of God,
offers Himself on the altar at Mass just as He did on Calvary. It is in a
different way, but it is the very same sacrifice.

We go to Mass every Sunday, and other days as well, to offer
this gift to the Father. We also offer up our hearts and lives to Him.
We offer all our joys and sufferings for His glory. We **worship** and
adore Him. Sometimes we sing joyous songs of praise that voice our
love.

At the beginning of the Mass, we make the Sign of the Cross. The
priest asks us to call to mind our sins, and to ask for God's
forgiveness. All together we say, "Lord have mercy. Christ have

102

mercy." We thank God for His goodness in another prayer which begins "Glory to God. . . ."

Next we listen to readings from the Bible. On Sundays the first reading is usually taken from the Old Testament, the second from an Epistle, or letter, that one of the Apostles wrote after Jesus returned to Heaven. These readings are messages of faith, hope, and love. They give us things to think about in our everyday lives.

After that, the priest reads to us from the Gospel. We stand during the Gospel reading because we are hearing Jesus' own words to us. For example, we might hear one of Jesus' parables, or stories, such as the Good Shepherd. At another Mass we may hear about one of Jesus' wonderful miracles. Every Sunday the **Gospel** gives us another message of love and hope. Remember, "Gospel" means Good News. The Good News of Christ's miracles, parables, and teachings is meant for us today, just as it was for His friends on earth two thousand years ago. The priest explains the Gospel message in a short talk called a homily. During the Gospel reading and the homily, it is very important to listen carefully.

After the homily, we stand with the priest to say the Creed. **Creed** means belief. Our Creed is a prayer that professes our faith. We say out loud that we believe in God the Father, the Creator of all things. We believe He sent His Son Jesus to save us from our sins. We believe God the Holy Spirit is alive among us. We say the Creed together at Mass because our faith is what binds us together as a Church.

At Mass Jesus comes into our hearts and lives in us. He teaches us through the readings. He offers Himself for us to God our Father. He unites Himself to us in Holy Communion. Truly, the Holy Mass is our greatest prayer on earth.

THE NICENE CREED

I believe in one God, the Father almighty, maker of heaven and earth, of all things visible and invisible.

I believe in one Lord Jesus Christ, the Only Begotten Son of God, born of the Father before all ages. God from God, Light from Light, true God from true God, begotten, not made, consubstantial with the Father; through him all things were made. For us men and for our salvation he came down from heaven,

and by the Holy Spirit was incarnate of the Virgin Mary, and became man.

For our sake he was crucified under Pontius Pilate, he suffered death and was buried, and rose again on the third day in accordance with the Scriptures. He ascended into heaven and is seated at the right hand of the Father. He will come again in glory to judge the living and the dead and his kingdom will have no end.

I believe in the Holy Spirit, the Lord, the giver of life, who proceeds from the Father and the Son, who with the Father and the Son is adored and glorified, who has spoken through the prophets.

I believe in one, holy, catholic, and apostolic Church. I confess one Baptism for the forgiveness of sins and I look forward to the resurrection of the dead and the life of the world to come. *Amen.*

Words to Know:

worship   Gospel   Creed

Q. 93 *Are we obliged to go to Mass?*
We are obliged to go to Mass on Sunday and on the Holy Days of Obligation. (CCC 2176–77).

Q. 94 *What is the most proper way of taking part in Mass?*
The most proper way of taking part in Mass is to offer it to God in union with the priest. We should remember the sacrifice of Jesus, His life, death, and Resurrection. We should receive Holy Communion (CCC 1391, 2180).

22   Offering Jesus To the Father

"He has no need, like those high priests, to offer sacrifices daily, first for his own sins and then for those of the people; he did this once for all when he offered up himself."

Hebrews 7:27

After we listen to God's Word and pray the Creed and the Prayers of the Faithful, we prepare our hearts for the most important part of the Mass. This is the moment when Jesus will offer His life to the Father once more through the hands of the priest.

First, we must prepare the gifts that go to the altar of God. We call this preparation time the **Offertory** of the Mass. During the Offertory, bread and wine are taken to the priest. These foods nourish us and keep us alive. By giving them to God, we show that we offer our very lives to Him. We offer Him our hearts. We offer Him all that we think, say, and do. We also offer money in the collection as a sign of our love for His people. All of these gifts are soon to be joined with Jesus, our best gift of all.

Honoring the coming of Jesus, we join with the angels in praising Him: "Holy, Holy, Holy Lord God of hosts. Heaven and earth are full of your glory. Hosanna in the highest. Blessed is he who comes in the name of the Lord. Hosanna in the highest."

Jesus is now about to come into our midst. Over the gifts of bread and wine, the priest says the words of Jesus at the Last Supper. "This is my Body. . . . This is the chalice of my Blood." This praying over the gifts is called the **Consecration**. At the moment of Consecration, the bread and wine change into Jesus' Body and Blood. The Precious Body of Jesus still looks, tastes, and feels like ordinary bread, but it is really and truly Jesus, our Savior. The Precious Blood still looks and tastes like ordinary wine, but it too is Jesus.

The priest takes the Sacred **Host** and lifts it up toward Heaven. We bow our heads because our Lord is really present before us. The priest then lifts up the chalice. We bow our heads again. God the Father accepts our offering held up by the priest. As He accepted both the earthly wheat and wine—the work of human hands—now He accepts the consecrated Body and Blood of His own Son, Jesus.

The Holy Eucharist is not only the best gift we can give the Father, it is the greatest treasure we have on earth. It is Jesus Himself among us. The **Eucharist** is not just a symbol of Jesus, but His real Body, Blood, Soul, and **Divinity**. Only the **appearances** of bread and wine remain. Appearance means how something looks. When the priest breaks the Host, Jesus is fully present in every broken part. If there are any extra consecrated Hosts after the Mass, the priest will treat them with special love and reverence and place them in the tabernacle. Once a Host is consecrated, anywhere in the world, it remains the Body, Blood, Soul, and Divinity of Jesus.

The Consecration of every Holy Mass renews Christ's gift on Calvary. Dying on the Cross, Jesus offered His life to the Father. Now at Mass, His life is offered to the Father through the priest and People of God. Through the Mass, Jesus keeps making up for our sins and uniting us with the Father just as He did in Jerusalem so long ago.

Words to Know:

Offertory	Consecration	Host
Eucharist	Divinity	appearance

Q. 95 *What is the Eucharist?*
The Eucharist is the Sacrament which contains the Body, Blood, Soul, and Divinity of our Lord Jesus Christ, really present under the appearances of bread and wine for the nourishment of souls (CCC 1323, 1333).

Q. 96 *When do the bread and wine become the Body and Blood of Jesus?*
The bread and wine become the Body and Blood of Jesus at the moment of the Consecration (CCC 1352–53).

Q. 97 *After the Consecration, is there nothing left of the bread and the wine?*
After the Consecration, neither bread nor wine is present any longer. Only the appearances of bread and wine, without their substance, remain (CCC 1375–76).

Q. 98 *When the Host is broken into several parts, is the Body of Jesus Christ broken?*
When the Host is broken into several parts, the Body of Jesus Christ is not broken, but only the appearances of the bread. The Body of our Lord remains whole and entire in each of the parts (CCC 1377).

Q. 99 *Is Jesus Christ found present in all the consecrated Hosts of the world?*
Yes, Jesus Christ is present in all the consecrated Hosts of the world (CCC 1380).

"I will go to the altar of God, to God my exceeding joy."

Psalm 43:4

23   The Bread of Life

"Truly, truly, I say to you, unless you eat the flesh of
the Son of man and drink his blood, you have no life
in you. . . ."

John 6:53

Jesus is the precious gift we offer the Father at Mass. Then we
receive Jesus into us as God's gift into our own souls. In this way, the
Sacrifice of the Mass truly forms a bond between Heaven and earth.

As we remember, in the Old Testament, people offered gifts of
value to God. A shepherd and his family might offer up a lamb. The
shepherd placed his lamb on an altar and killed it. This was a sign that
his gift was completely offered to God. But something else was
needed to complete the act of love. The shepherd and his family sat
together and ate the lamb as a sacred meal. This was an important sign
of their covenant, or friendship, with God. They wanted to be closer to
Him by eating something that had been offered and He had accepted.

Under the New Covenant, we lift up the Lamb of God. Then we
share in this sacrificial gift by receiving God's own Son in Holy
Communion. The priest holds Him before us and says, "Behold the
Lamb of God, behold him who takes away the sins of the world.
Blessed are those called to the supper of the Lamb." We look at Jesus
and answer, "Lord, I am not **worthy** that you should enter under my
roof, but only say the word and my soul shall be healed." To share
fully in the New Covenant or the full friendship with God, we must
share in Jesus' sacrifice and the meal of the sacrifice.

The Eucharist really nourishes us. Just as we need food for our
bodies to keep us alive, growing, and strong, so we need food for our
souls. The Eucharist, the Bread of Life, does this. It keeps the life of

112

"As often as you eat this bread and drink the chalice, you proclaim the Lord's death until he comes."

1 Corinthians 11:26

grace alive in our hearts. It helps us to grow as good and loving children of God. Jesus said, "Whoever eats of this Bread will never hunger." He also told us that by eating this Bread we will never die; we shall live for ever.

Sharing this sacred banquet unites us in friendship with the Father. It also binds all of us together as one. Our faith in the one true God makes us a family. All over the world, members of God's family gather to worship the way Jesus taught us at the Last Supper. Whenever we do this in memory of Him, we give joy to the Father. We become more and more like His beloved Son in Whom He is well pleased.

Words to Know:

Communion   worthy

Because there is one bread, we who are many are one body, for we all partake of the one bread.

1 Corinthians 10:17

Q. 100 *What is the New Covenant?*

The New Covenant is the perfect and unbreakable friendship to which man is called by God. Jesus established the New Covenant for us. He is the sacrifice and meal that seals the New Covenant. We are called to share in the New Covenant through Holy Communion (CCC 610–11).

We Pray:

O Sacrament most holy, O Sacrament divine,
All praise and all thanksgiving be every moment Thine.

24 Jesus Comes to Us in the Holy Eucharist

"Because there is one bread, we who are many are one body, for we all partake of the one bread."

1 Corinthians 10:17

Jesus once changed five loaves and two fishes into food for five thousand people. This miracle of love amazed His followers. But later, Jesus promised them a far more wonderful bread. He explained that this heavenly bread would satisfy the hungers of the heart. Then He told them: "I am the Bread of Life. He who eats My Flesh and drinks My Blood will live for ever."

The Holy Eucharist is the Bread of Life that Jesus promised. We are very blessed because we can receive it at every Mass. Whenever we do, Jesus comes as a Guest into our hearts.

To prepare for our divine Guest, three things are necessary. We must believe in Him. We must be in His good graces, which means that if we have a grave sin on our soul, we must go to Confession before receiving the Eucharist. We must not eat or drink anything (except water or medicine) for one hour before He comes to us. These things prepare us properly to receive Jesus in Holy Communion.

Once we receive Jesus, we kneel down to make a **thanksgiving**. Thanksgiving just means giving thanks. We may close our eyes to give Him our full attention. We silently pray to Him and He listens. Jesus already knows us completely, but He is pleased when we share our lives with Him. During Holy Communion we can tell Him our disappointments and joys, our hopes and dreams. If we are having

"My flesh is food indeed, and my blood is drink indeed. He who eats my flesh and drinks my blood, abides in me, and I in him."

John 6:56–57

trouble being kind or good, Jesus understands. He will help us. If we want to be more obedient at home or school, we can ask Him to show us the way.

Every time Jesus comes to us, He fills our souls with His own life. We become more and more like Him. He gives us the strength to be generous, forgiving, and kind. We become the grace-filled persons God created us to be.

When we love someone, we never get tired of his company. We spend as much time with that person as we can. Think of how much more we want to enjoy the company of Jesus. The best way to stay close to Jesus is to go to Mass and receive Holy Communion, even every day if possible. He is the food and life of our souls. If we share in His life on earth, He will one day invite us to live with Him for ever in Heaven.

> "Your fathers ate the manna in the wilderness, and they died. This is the bread which comes down from heaven, that a man may eat of it and not die. I am the living bread which came down from heaven; if any one eats of this bread, he will live for ever; and the bread which I shall give for the life of the world is my flesh."
>
> John 6:49–51

Word to Know:

thanksgiving

Q. 101 *What things are necessary for the worthy reception of Holy Communion?*
For a worthy reception of Holy Communion three things are necessary: first, to be in the grace of God; second, to realize and to consider Whom we are about to receive; third, to observe the Eucharistic fast (CCC 1385–88).

Q. 102 *Is it a good and useful thing to receive Holy Communion frequently?*
It is a very good thing and most useful to receive Holy Communion frequently, even every day, provided it is done always in the right way (CCC 1391–92).

Q. 103 *What effects does the Eucharist produce in him who receives Jesus worthily?*
In him who receives Jesus worthily, the Holy Eucharist preserves and increases grace, which is the life of the soul, just as food does for the life of the body. The Holy Eucharist takes away venial sins and helps us avoid mortal sins. It gives spiritual joy and consolation by increasing charity and the hope of eternal life, of which it is the pledge (CCC 1394–95).

25 Jesus Rises in Splendor

"In my Father's house are many rooms; if it were not so, would I have told you that I go to prepare a place for you? And when I go and prepare a place for you, I will come again and will take you to myself, that where I am you may be also."

John 14:2–3

Early on the Sunday morning after Jesus died, some women went to anoint His Sacred Body with spices and oils. But they arrived to find an empty tomb. The heavy stone that had sealed it was rolled away, and the Body of Jesus was nowhere in sight. A beautiful angel told the women Jesus was no longer dead, but alive. "He is risen!" the angel said. "Rejoice and tell the others!"

The women ran to find the Apostles and tell them the news. Even though Jesus had told His friends that He would rise on the third day after His death, they were surprised. They wanted to see with their own eyes. Peter and John ran to the tomb and trembled with excitement to see that it was true. Only the burial cloths remained. Jesus had risen from the dead. He was alive!

We are told that the first person to whom Jesus appeared was Mary Magdalene, the holy woman, whose many sins He had forgiven. She was weeping in the garden near the tomb because she missed Him. Jesus softly called her by name. She looked up and cried, "Teacher!" Jesus also appeared to two disciples who were walking sadly in the country. Once the men realized it was Jesus, alive and well, they too raced to tell the Apostles.

Soon after, the Apostles, who were some of Jesus' **disciples**, were gathered together in an upper room. The doors were locked. Suddenly

Jesus appeared among them! At first, the Apostles were afraid Jesus might be a ghost. But Jesus reassured them. "Peace be with you," He said. Then He ate with them. Their joy was great.

The Apostle named Thomas doubted that Jesus had risen from the dead. He was not with the others right after Jesus rose from the dead. He said, "Unless I see in His hands the print of the nails, touch them, and put my hand into His side, I will not believe."

When Jesus appeared in the upper room, He looked straight at Thomas. He said, "Put your finger here; look, here are My hands. Give me your hand; put it into My side, and believe." Thomas did so and then answered in awe, "My Lord and my God."

Jesus said: "Because you have seen Me, you believe. Blessed are those who have not seen, and yet have believed." Jesus was speaking about all of us. One day He will reward us for our faith.

Jesus taught us by His life, death, and Resurrection that our suffering and death will be turned into glory and everlasting life. On **Good Friday**, He suffered and died on the Cross. But on Easter Sunday He arose from the dead in full splendor. Every **Easter**, we celebrate this miracle of the **Resurrection**: Jesus rising from the dead. We rejoice because Jesus' sacrifice on the Cross destroyed death. Each of us will die one day, but our death will be a doorway to Heaven. We will be alive for ever just like Jesus, our Risen Lord.

"Go therefore and make disciples of all nations, baptizing them in the name of the Father and of the Son and of the Holy Spirit . . . and behold, I am with you always, to the close of the age."

Matthew 28:19–20

After He rose from the dead, Jesus stayed among His disciples for forty days. He taught them more about the Faith and their mission on earth. He told Peter, the first Pope, to "feed My sheep." He taught all of them to go out to teach and baptize. He promised He would send the Holy Spirit to help them.

Finally it was time for Jesus to go home to Heaven. "I am with you always, to the close of the age," He promised. Then He ascended to Heaven and into glory. Jesus, the King of Heaven and earth, has prepared a place for us in Heaven, too. That is why, no matter what happens to us on this earth, we can be full of joy and hope.

Words to Know:

disciple   Good Friday   Easter   Resurrection

Q. 104 *What is the Resurrection?*
The Resurrection is the fact that Christ is risen from the dead and has conquered death. Jesus rose from the dead on the first Easter Sunday, on the third day after his death on the Cross. The Resurrection is the crowning truth of our Faith (CCC 638, 640–41).

Q. 105 *How can we know that our suffering and death will be turned into glory and everlasting life?*
Jesus' Resurrection proves Jesus' works and teachings, His power and divine authority. By Jesus' death, we are freed from sin and death. By Jesus' rising from the dead, the way to new life is opened for us (CCC 651, 654).

Q. 106 *Why did Jesus make Peter the first Pope?*
Jesus made Peter the first Pope so that Peter and the Apostles with him could rule and govern the Church according to Jesus' will and teachings (CCC 816).

Q. 107 *Why did Jesus send His Apostles to teach and baptize all people?*
Jesus sent the Apostles to teach and baptize all people so that all people could share in Jesus' life through the Church (CCC 1213, 1229, 1257).

Q. 108 *What was the Ascension?*
The Ascension was the moment when Jesus rose bodily into Heaven to sit at the Father's right hand. The Ascension happened forty days after the Resurrection (CCC 659, 663).

WE PRAY TO GOD AT MASS:

To our departed brothers and sisters and to all who were pleasing to you at their passing from this life, give kind admittance to your kingdom.

124

26 The Coming of The Holy Spirit

"And the Spirit of the LORD shall rest upon him, the spirit of wisdom and understanding, the spirit of counsel and might, the spirit of knowledge and the fear of the LORD."

Isaiah 11:2

After Jesus rose up to Heaven on **Ascension** Thursday, the Apostles prayed and waited with Mary. They all stayed together in one home. Ten days later, a strong wind suddenly swept through the house. A bright flame of fire appeared over each one. These wonderful signs happened as the **Holy Spirit**, Who is God, the Third Person of the Blessed Trinity, came into their hearts. The Holy Spirit filled them with courage and love.

The people outside heard the wind and gathered to listen. Peter and the other Apostles came out of the house in great excitement. They were full of joy and hope. The Holy Spirit created in them such a deep desire to carry on Jesus' work, that they began preaching at once. The Holy Spirit also gave them the power to speak in a way that all people could understand them. Men, women, and children of many countries and languages discovered the Good News that day for the first time.

Peter called out, "Men of Judea and all you who dwell in Jerusalem, hear these words: Jesus of Nazareth was a man sent among you by God. You know this by His miracles, signs, and wonders. God allowed Him to be crucified on a Cross. But now He has raised Him up again. We have seen Him. And now, from Heaven, He has poured out the Holy Spirit as His Father promised."

"What must we do?" the people asked. Peter answered, "Repent and be baptized, every one of you, in the name of Jesus Christ for the forgiveness of your sins, and you will receive the gift of the Holy Spirit. This promise is for you and your children, and for all those, everywhere, whom the Lord Our God calls to Himself." That **Pentecost** Sunday, three thousand people were baptized and the Church was born.

We do not hear a great wind or see tongues of fire, but the Holy Spirit is with us, too. He came to live in us on the day we were baptized. That is why we call ourselves temples of the Holy Spirit. We are His dwelling place.

Like mirrors we reflect the glory of the Lord. We grow brighter and brighter as we are changed into the image of Jesus. This is the work of the Holy Spirit.

adapted from 2 Corinthians 3:18

"The fruit of the Spirit is love, joy, peace, patience, kindness, goodness, faithfulness."

Galatians 5:22

Like the people baptized on Pentecost Sunday, we receive gifts from the Holy Spirit. The Holy Spirit teaches all truth and helps us to understand our lessons about our Faith. He inspires us to love others, even when it is hard. He helps us to know and be sorry for our sins. He gives us the grace to be both strong and gentle like Jesus. He is with us always, wherever we go.

Words to Know:

Ascension   Holy Spirit   Pentecost

Q. 109 *What is Pentecost?*
Pentecost was the day when the Holy Spirit was poured out upon the hiding Apostles, bringing God's life to the Church. Pentecost happened ten days after the Ascension (CCC 731, 739).

Q. 110 *What is the role of the Holy Spirit in the Church?*
The Holy Spirit completes the mission of Jesus in the Church. The Holy Spirit prepares men to draw people to communion with God (CCC 737).

Q. 111 *When did you receive the Holy Spirit?*
I received the Holy Spirit when I was baptized
(CCC 1257).

SONG OF PRAISE

Come, Holy Ghost, Creator blest,
    And in our hearts take up Your rest.
Come with Your grace and heavenly aid
    To fill the hearts which You have made.

Come, Holy Spirit, fill the hearts of Your faithful, and kindle in them the fire of Your love.

27   God's Family on Earth

"Now you are the body of Christ and individually members of it."

1 Corinthians 12:27

Jesus founded the **Church** on earth, and He is her King. But before He ascended into Heaven, He asked His Apostles to spend the rest of their lives continuing His work. He gave them the power to teach and to guide the Church. He asked them to follow His footsteps in bringing truth, love, and grace into the world.

All of the Apostles embraced this mission, but Peter's mission was even greater. One day Jesus told him, "You are Peter and upon this rock I will build My Church. And the gates of Hell shall not prevail against it. I will entrust to you the keys of the Kingdom of Heaven. Whatever you declare bound on earth will be bound in Heaven."

With these words, Jesus invited Peter to take His place on earth. Peter accepted Christ's call. He became the first Pope, the head of the whole Church. Ever since that time, the Church has had an unbroken line of Popes to lead and guide her. We call the Pope the Vicar of Christ because he represents Jesus. Jesus Himself gave him that power. That is why Catholics everywhere respect and obey him.

The Pope is also the head of bishops all over the world. A bishop is like the Good Shepherd that Jesus spoke of in the Gospel. He watches over his flock, protecting it from danger. Today thousands of bishops all over the world carry on the work of the Apostles. They teach, preach, and guide. They deliver the message of Jesus. They explain the rules of the Church. They tell us how to avoid sin and lead good lives.

130

"I am the vine, you are the branches."

John 15:5

Each bishop has the help of many priests. Priests are very important to the Church because they bring us the grace of the Sacraments. They share in the God-given power to forgive sins and offer Holy Mass. We are blessed to have priests in our parishes, schools, and neighborhoods. Jesus comes into our lives through them.

Other priests bring the light of Christ to faraway parts of the earth. They are joined by **religious** sisters and brothers who want to give their whole lives to God by teaching and helping others. They are called **missionaries**. They make the Church rich in blessings by their sacrifices and love.

Bishops, priests, sisters, and brothers are called by God to serve the Church in a special way. God calls all of us to do special things in the Church, too. When we go to Mass every Sunday to pray and worship, we are answering God's call. When we learn about His Word and obey His Commandments, we are serving and loving Him. God wants parents and children and other people in the world to build up His Kingdom just as He calls priests and religious brothers and sisters. We are called the laity of the Church. We are baptized, believing members of God's family.

The laity help the bishops and priests in bringing the Word of God to all people. Sometimes in doing this work people are asked to offer their lives. We call these people **martyrs**. Faith in Christ means so much to them that they risk even death to proclaim it. Jesus said that when men persecute His followers for His name's sake, He will bless His followers with great reward in Heaven.

All of us are destined for Heaven. If we lead a good life on earth, God will take us to be with Him forever. Members of God's family who have died and now live in Heaven are called saints. The saints were ordinary people, but they loved God with all their hearts and souls. This is the secret of how all of us, no matter what we do in the Church, can become saints.

Saint Paul told us that our Church is like a body with many parts. Whenever one small part is hurt, the whole body suffers. For example, we need our eyes to see, our lungs to breathe, and our feet to walk. If any one of these were taken away, our whole body would suffer the loss. So it is with our Church. Christ is the head and we make up all the other parts. Our good actions and prayers build up the health and strength of the whole Church. All of us are one united body under Christ.

This is why the Church is called **Catholic**. Catholic means "universal" or "for all." Christ founded the Church for everyone. Today because of good priests, missionaries, and lay people, the Church has spread to all nations. Even though we may never see these people in faraway lands, we are one with them because we share the same beliefs. We are all part of God's family on earth—the Catholic Church.

Words to Know:

Church   religious
missionary   martyr   Catholic

Q. 112 *Who founded the Church?*
Jesus Christ founded the Church. Jesus gathered His faithful followers into one society, placed it under the direction of the Apostles with Saint Peter as its head, and gave it its sacrifice, its Sacraments, and the Holy Spirit, Who gives it life (CCC 763–65).

Q. 113 *Who are the pastors of the Church?*
The pastors of the Church are the Pope and the bishops united with him (CCC 816, 881).

Q. 114 *Who is the Pope?*
The Pope is the successor of Saint Peter as Bishop of Rome. The Pope is the visible head of the entire Church (CCC 882).

"If you continue in my word, you are truly my disciples, and you will know the truth, and the truth will make you free."

John 8:31–32

134

28 Our Life in the Church

"My sheep hear my voice, and I know them, and they
follow me; and I give them eternal life, and they shall
never perish, and no one shall snatch them out of my
hand."

John 10:27–28

Signs help us every day of our life. Often they call our attention to
important things we cannot see or hear. Smoke is a sign of fire. Red
lights or sirens are signs of danger. A heart is a sign of love.

We cannot see love. It is invisible. But love is real. We can show it
to others through our actions. For example, your mother may show
you her love by kind words, a hug, or a smile. Hearing, feeling, or
seeing these signs helps you to understand the love in your mother's
heart. Without signs, her love would be hidden. With signs, you see
and understand the wonderful gift that you are receiving.

In the Church, Jesus gave us signs of His grace in the seven
Sacraments. A **Sacrament** is a sign. It uses things we can see and hear
to tell us about something else that we cannot see or hear. Jesus and
His grace are hidden from our eyes, but we know He is present in
every Sacrament. Jesus promised this when He instituted these
Sacraments during His public life on earth. He wanted to leave us
visible signs of His grace being poured out to us.

The first Sacrament we receive is Baptism. The signs of this
Sacrament are words and water. Most of us were baptized when we
were little babies. Our parents and godparents took us to church. They
made our baptismal promises for us because we were too young to
speak. Then the priest poured water over our heads. He called us by

name and said, "I baptize you in the Name of the Father and of the Son and of the Holy Spirit."

At that very moment, we became **Christians**: baptized followers of Christ. Our sin was washed away and our souls were filled with brilliant new life. This new life in our soul was God's own life, called grace. God shared grace with us on our Baptism day so that we could be His own precious children forever. He welcomed us with open arms into His family on earth. Because of our Baptism, He can one day welcome us with open arms into His Kingdom in Heaven.

As a result of our Baptism, we can spend the rest of our life keeping the life of grace alive in our soul. God understands us completely, so He knows that we need special help to do this. That is why He gave us the other Sacraments: to keep God's grace. In this way, He can keep pouring His life and love into our hearts.

In the Sacrament of the Holy Eucharist, He gives us His own Son as food for our souls. Bread, wine, and the words of the priest are our signs that Jesus is present. Once the priest changes the bread and wine into Jesus' own Body and Blood, we can receive Him into our hearts. If we receive this Sacrament often, the life of grace in our soul grows more and more strong.

In the Sacrament of Penance, God gives us the chance to win back grace that we have lost in sin. We know God is really present, because we have the sign of the priest's healing, forgiving words. When he says to us, "I absolve you from your sins in the Name of the Father and of the Son and of the Holy Spirit," Jesus Himself speaks through him, forgiving and blessing us.

When we receive the Sacrament of Confirmation, the Holy Spirit fills us with the grace to be even stronger members of the Church. This Sacrament will help us to do whatever God asks us as members of His family.

RENEWAL OF BAPTISMAL PROMISES

Do you renounce Satan?

  I do.

And all his works?

  I do.

And all his empty show?

  I do.

Do you renounce sin, so as to live in the freedom of the children of God?

  I do.

Do you renounce the lure of evil, so that sin may have no mastery over you?

  I do.

Do you renounce Satan, the author and prince of sin?

  I do.

Do you believe in God, the Father almighty, the Creator of heaven and earth?

  I do.

Do you believe in Jesus Christ, his only Son, our Lord, who was born of the Virgin Mary, suffered death and was buried, rose again from the dead and is seated at the right hand of the Father?

  I do.

Do you believe in the Holy Spirit, the holy Catholic Church, the communion of saints, the forgiveness of sins, the resurrection of the body, and life everlasting?

  I do.

And may almighty God, the Father of our Lord Jesus Christ, who has given us new birth by water and the Holy Spirit and bestowed on us forgiveness of our sins, keep us by his grace, in Christ Jesus our Lord, for eternal life. *Amen.*

Later in life, we may receive some of the other Sacraments: Holy Orders, Matrimony (Marriage), and the Anointing of the Sick. The important thing to remember is that God gave us the Sacraments as a special invitation to share in His life. Receiving them strengthens our friendship with Him and unites us to Him. If we live up to the grace we receive in the Sacraments, we really will begin to think, speak, and act like Christ. His own life will shine out of us.

When we are full of God's grace, it is easier to keep our promises to God and follow His Commandments. We love Him so much we want to go to Mass every Sunday, we want to practice our faith and witness it to others. We want to love God most of all, and love our neighbor as ourselves.

Prayer is one of the greatest ways we can show our love of our neighbor. God wants us to pray, not only for those in His family, the Church, but also for others who do not have the gift of faith. Jesus told the Apostles that He came for everyone. He loves all people. He wants everyone in the world to belong to His family. Even if we cannot join the missionaries in distant lands, we can join them with our prayers. Prayer is powerful, and our prayers for people who do not yet know and love God can bring them closer to Him. Jesus said, "They will know you are My disciples by your love." To be His followers, we must love and pray for all the world.

Words to Know:

Sacrament   Christian

Q. 115 *What are the Sacraments?*
The Sacraments are signs of grace instituted by Jesus Christ to make us holy (CCC 1114, 1116, 1127).

Q. 116 *How do the Sacraments make us holy?*
The Sacraments make us holy either by giving us the first sanctifying grace, which takes away sin, or by increasing that grace which we already possess (CCC 1123).

Q. 117 *What are the seven Sacraments?*
The seven Sacraments are: Baptism, Confirmation, Eucharist, Penance, Anointing of the Sick, Matrimony, and Holy Orders (CCC 1113).

". . . Put on love, which binds everything together in perfect harmony. And let the peace of Christ rule in your hearts, to which indeed you were called in the one body."

Colossians 3:14–15

140

29   Mary, Our Mother And Queen

"When Jesus saw his mother, and the disciple whom he loved standing near, he said to his mother, 'Woman, behold, your son!' Then he said to the disciple, 'Behold, your mother!' And from that hour the disciple took her to his own home."

John 19:26–27

Jesus asked Mary, His own Mother, to be our Mother too on the day she and Saint John stood at the foot of His Cross. "Mother," He said, "behold your son. Son, behold your Mother." With that, Mary inherited many, many children—the whole Church!

Mary actually became the Mother of the Church long before that, as a young woman who bravely said yes to God's plan. She was free to say no. But she wanted to do whatever God asked. Because of her trust, obedience, and love, Jesus came into the world as a little Child. He would become our Savior. Mary helped God keep His promise to His people. Her choice brought salvation and light to the world.

God prepared Mary in a very special way for her role in our salvation. He allowed her to be the one person in the world, besides Jesus, who was conceived without Original Sin. In other words, Mary never needed to be baptized like all of us. We were born with the effects of our first parents' sin. But Mary was born with no trace of sin. That is why she is called the **Immaculate Conception**. She came into the world already filled with God's life. That is why the angel Gabriel approached her with the words, "Hail Mary, **full of grace**."

141

Mary brought Jesus into our world, and she lived her whole life without sin. That is why she holds the highest place in Heaven after her Son. Just as she brought Jesus to us, so she brings us to Jesus. Sometimes Mary appears on earth with a message from Him. Usually the message is to stop sinning, to love God, and to pray. She tells us these things as a loving Mother, inspiring us gently to be good.

We are wise to ask Mary to pray for us, because Jesus always listens to His Mother. His first miracle at the wedding feast in Cana happened at her request. She told Him, "Son, they have no wine." Jesus had not planned to work a miracle that day, but Mary's request won over His heart. He changed six jars of water into delicious wine for the guests of the bride and groom. Just like the couple in Cana, we can go to Mary for help. We can ask her to tell Jesus what we need. Then we can patiently wait for His generous love to answer.

We please God when we try to imitate the virtues of Mary. Mary's greatest desire was to do His will, and she did it in each hour of her life. In Nazareth, she did His will by keeping a happy, comfortable home for Jesus and Joseph. At the foot of the Cross, she did His will in quiet, helpless suffering. After the feast of Pentecost, she did His will by helping the Apostles build the early Church.

Now Mary is the Queen of Heaven, but she still does whatever God wills. His will is that she remain a loving Mother in our lives, leading us to Jesus and our heavenly home.

Words to Know:

Immaculate Conception   full of grace

142

Our Lady has appeared to her children on earth many times. Each time, she brings a special message to build our hope and faith. In the winter of 1531, Mary appeared in Mexico to a humble man named Juan Diego. In this apparition, we call the Mother of God "Our Lady of Guadalupe." Mary's words to Juan Diego are meant for each one of us:

"Hear me, my dear little child. Let nothing discourage you or make you sad. Do not be afraid of illness, worry, or pain. Am I not here, your Mother? Have I not put you on my lap and sheltered you in my arms? Are you not tucked in the folds of my mantle? Is there anything else you need?"

These words show us that Mary cares for us with the heart of a loving Mother. If we honor and obey her, she will never leave us in this life. She will help us be happy on earth and find our way home to Heaven.

Q. 118 *What was the Immaculate Conception?*
The Immaculate Conception was a unique gift from God to prepare Mary to be the Mother of Jesus. Mary was "full of grace" and free from Original Sin from the first moment of her existence (CCC 490–91).

144

30 The Communion of Saints

"What no eye has seen, nor ear heard, nor the heart of man conceived, what God has prepared for those who love him. . . ."

1 Corinthians 2:9

Jesus taught us that death is not the end of life, but its real beginning. Death is the doorway to Heaven. Jesus made this possible by His sacrifice on the Cross. His gift of Himself to the Father was so pleasing that it destroyed death, earning us the gift of eternal life. People who live with God in Heaven after they die are called saints. God welcomes the saints into glorious and everlasting happiness.

While Jesus' death on the Cross opened the gates of Heaven, we must do our part to live there one day. The saints earned their heavenly reward. They loved God and kept His Laws. They found many ways to know, love, and serve Him during their lives. They were human, so sometimes they sinned or made mistakes. But they came to God, told Him they were sorry, and started all over again. Some of the greatest saints in Heaven, like Mary Magdalene, Saint Paul, and Saint Augustine, were sinners for a long, long time. But each one finally turned to God and gave Him his whole heart. This love turned them from great sinners into great saints.

Many people who love God and die in His friendship are not fully ready for Heaven. First they go to **Purgatory** to be cleansed of their venial sins. Souls in Purgatory suffer because they miss God, but the suffering is mixed with joy because they know they will see Him soon. We can help the souls in Purgatory reach Heaven faster by offering our Masses, prayers, and sacrifices for them.

The saints in Heaven, the souls in Purgatory, and the members of the Church on earth make up the whole family of God's people. We call our one great family the **Communion of Saints**. This Communion of Saints can love and help each other across the barriers of time. Even though the saints are in Heaven, and we are on earth, we can call on them for prayers and help. Even though the souls in Purgatory seem so far away, our prayers make us close to them.

One day this world we live in will come to an end. God will gather all of the people who have ever lived and judge each one. That day will be the **Last Judgment**. On that day our good actions will be like treasures. God will see them and He will offer us back a crown of glory. Jesus will say, "Come, you who have My Father's blessing. Inherit the Kingdom prepared for you from the beginning of the world!"

We can look forward to this day of rejoicing by preparing our hearts now, today, on earth. We must always keep our eyes and hearts on Heaven because that is our true home. We will get there if we keep knowing, loving, and serving God, our King and final destiny.

Words to Know:

Purgatory   Communion of Saints   Last Judgment

Q. 119 *What does "Communion of Saints" mean?*
The *Communion of Saints* means all the faithful who form one single body in Jesus Christ: the victorious souls in Heaven, the suffering souls in Purgatory, and the militant souls on earth (CCC 947, 954).

"Our hearts are made for You, O Lord, and will not rest until they rest in You."

Saint Augustine

Words to Know

Abraham: the father of God's Chosen People.

all-perfect: without fault or defect.

anoint: to put oil on someone as a sign that God is giving His strength or power to that person.

appearance: how something looks.

Ascension: when Jesus went back to Heaven forty days after He rose from the dead.

Baptism: the Sacrament which takes away Original Sin. It gives us God's grace, incorporates us into Christ, and makes us children of God.

bear false witness: to lie about someone.

Bethlehem: the town where Jesus was born.

Bible: the holy book God gave us. It tells about God's love for us, His Chosen People, about the Savior He sent, and about the early days of the Church.

bishop: a man who does the work of the Apostles and takes care of a large group of Catholics.

Calvary: the hilltop where Jesus died.

Canaan: the Promised Land God gave to the Israelites.

Catholic: a member of the Catholic Church.

Christian: a baptized follower of Jesus Christ.

Church, the: the group of followers of Jesus who believe the same Faith, receive the Sacraments, and obey the Pope; another name for the family of God.

Commandments: God's Laws, or rules for His Kingdom.

Communion: *see* Eucharist.

Communion of Saints: the unity of all the members of the Church here on earth with those in Heaven and in Purgatory.

Consecration: the part of the Mass when the priest changes the bread and wine into the Body and Blood of Jesus.

contrition: sorrow for sin.

covenant: a promise or agreement between two or more persons or groups. God made a covenant with the Israelites, His Chosen People.

covet: to desire something wrongfully which does not belong to you.

create: to make something out of nothing.

Creator: God, the Maker of all things.

Creed: a prayer telling what we believe.

David: the boy who killed Goliath and grew up to be a king of Israel. Jesus descended from the family of David.

disciple: a follower of Jesus.

divinity: the nature of God.

Easter: the day on which Jesus rose from the dead.

Eucharist: the Sacrament in which Jesus comes to us in the appearance of bread and wine; the Body and Blood of Jesus.

examination of conscience: thinking about what we did to see if it was good or bad in preparation for Confession.

faith: a gift from God by which we believe in Him and everything He teaches us.

Fall, the: the sin of our first parents, Adam and Eve.

forgiveness: the act of pardoning someone who has done something wrong.

foster father: a man who takes the place of the real father.

full of grace: all holy, being free from sin. This was the angel's greeting to Mary.

Goliath: a gigantic Philistine soldier whom David killed.

Good Friday: the day Jesus suffered and died for us.

good will: always wanting to do what is right.

Gospel: the "Good News"; the story of the life, death, and Resurrection of Jesus.

grace: the life of God in our souls. We receive grace from the Sacraments, from prayer, and from doing good works.

Heaven: the place of perfect happiness with God for ever. Heaven is for those who have asked God to forgive their sins and who have died in His love.

Holy Day of Obligation: a special feast day, besides Sunday, when Catholics are required to participate at Mass and not do unnecessary work.

Holy Spirit: God, the Third Person of the Blessed Trinity.

Holy Thursday: the day Jesus gave us the Holy Eucharist for the first time.

honesty: truthfulness.

honor: to love, respect, and obey.

Host: the round wafer of bread used at Mass. At the Consecration it is changed into Jesus, the Bread of Life.

humble: not proud.

Immaculate Conception: the special gift God gave to the Blessed Virgin Mary of being free from Original Sin from the first moment of her life.

infinite: without end.

John the Baptist: a cousin of Jesus. John was the last of the prophets. He helped prepare the people for the coming of Jesus.

king: a man who rules a kingdom.

Last Judgment: the event at the end of the world at which God will judge our lives.

Last Supper: the dinner Jesus had with the Twelve Apostles the night before He died. At the Last Supper Jesus gave us the Holy Eucharist.

Lord: a name for Jesus because He is the King of the universe.

manger: a box that holds feed for animals.

martyr: a person who dies for his faith in Jesus.

Mass: the sacrifice of Jesus on the Cross offered by the priest in our church and in every Catholic church.

miracle: something wonderful that is done by the power of God. It is something that only God can do.

missionary: a person who works to spread the Good News of Jesus in every part of the world.

mortal sin: a very big sin that kills all life of grace in a soul.

Moses: a leader and prophet of the Israelites; God gave the people the Ten Commandments through him.

Mount Sinai: the mountain on which God made a covenant with the Israelites and gave the Ten Commandments.

New Testament: the second part of the Bible. It tells us about the life and teachings of Jesus and the early Church.

obey: to do what we are told.

Offertory: the part of the Mass where bread and wine are brought to the altar and offered as a gift to God.

Old Testament: the first part of the Bible. It tells the history and preparation of God's Chosen People for the coming of the Savior.

Original Sin: the first sin, committed when Adam and Eve disobeyed God. We are all born with Original Sin on our souls.

parable: a story that teaches a lesson.

Passion: the suffering and death of Jesus to free us from sin.

penance: a prayer we say or something we do to help make up for our sins.

Pentecost: the coming of the Spirit to the Apostles.

Pharaoh: a ruler in ancient Egypt.

Pope: the chief leader and teacher of the Catholic Church who takes the place of Jesus on earth.

prayer: the lifting of the heart and mind to God; talking with God.

prophet: a man who prepared the people for the coming of the Savior.

Purgatory: the place where a soul goes to be made clean from all venial sin and receive the punishment due to sins already forgiven before it can go to Heaven.

purity: cleanness in thought, word, and act.

redeem: to buy back; to free someone by buying freedom for him.

religious: men and women who are dedicated to God in a special way.

remembrance: in memory of someone or something.

respect: to think highly of.

Resurrection: when Jesus rose from the dead.

reverent: showing respect.

Sacrament: a sign given by Jesus that gives us grace.

Sacrament of Penance: the Sacrament in which all sins committed after Baptism are forgiven; also called Confession or Reconciliation.

sacrifice: something that is offered to God. At Mass we offer Jesus to God the Father as a sacrifice for our sins.

saint: a holy person who loved God very much on earth and now is in Heaven.

Savior: Jesus Christ, who died to save us all from sin.

sin: any wrong we do on purpose. Sin turns us away from God.

sorrow for sins: being sorry for and regretting what we have done wrong.

stable: a place where farm animals eat and sleep.

superstition: thinking that ordinary things have powers that only God has.

Temple: the building in Jerusalem where the Jews worshiped God.

thanksgiving: giving thanks.

trust: to depend on or hope in.

truth: the way things actually are.

venial sin: a small sin that makes a soul weak and less pleasing to God.

vow: a free promise we make to God.

worship: love, honor, and adoration which we give to God.

worthy: having value, being deserving.

We Pray

THE SIGN OF THE CROSS

In the Name of the Father, and of the Son, and of the Holy Spirit. *Amen.*

OUR FATHER

Our Father, Who art in Heaven, hallowed be Thy Name; Thy Kingdom come; Thy will be done on earth as it is in Heaven. Give us this day our daily bread, and forgive us our trespasses as we forgive those who trespass against us; and lead us not into temptation, but deliver us from evil. *Amen.*

HAIL MARY

Hail Mary, full of grace! The Lord is with thee. Blessed art thou among women, and blessed is the fruit of thy womb, Jesus. Holy Mary, Mother of God, pray for us sinners, now and at the hour of our death. *Amen.*

GLORY BE

Glory be to the Father, and to the Son, and to the Holy Spirit, as it was in the beginning, is now, and ever shall be, world without end. *Amen.*

PRAYER BEFORE MEALS

Bless us O Lord, and these Thy gifts, which we are about to receive, from Thy bounty, through Christ, our Lord. *Amen.*

APOSTLES' CREED

I believe in God,
    the Father almighty,
    Creator of heaven and earth,
    and in Jesus Christ,
    his only Son, our Lord,
    who was conceived by
    the Holy Spirit,
    born of the Virgin Mary,
    suffered under Pontius Pilate,
    was crucified, died, and was buried;
    he descended into hell;
    on the third day he rose again from the dead;
    he ascended into heaven,
    and is seated at the right
    hand of God the Father almighty;
    from there he will come to judge
    the living and the dead.

I believe in the Holy Spirit,
    the holy catholic Church,
    the communion of saints,
    the forgiveness of sins,
    the resurrection of the body,
    and life everlasting.

Amen.

MORNING OFFERING

O Jesus through the Immaculate Heart of Mary I offer You my prayers, works, joys, and sufferings of this day in union with the Holy Sacrifice of the Mass.

I offer them for all the intentions of your Sacred Heart: for the salvation of souls, reparation for sin, the reunion of all Christians.

I offer them for all the intentions of our Bishops and all Apostles of Prayer and in particular for those recommended by our Holy Father this month. *Amen.*

ACT OF FAITH

O my God, I firmly believe that You are one God in three Divine Persons: Father, Son, and Holy Spirit. I believe that Your divine Son became man and died for our sins, and that He will come to judge the living and the dead. I believe these and all the truths which the Holy Catholic Church teaches, because You revealed them, Who can neither deceive nor be deceived. *Amen.*

ACT OF HOPE

O my God, relying on Your infinite goodness and promises, I hope to obtain pardon of my sins, the help of Your grace, and life everlasting, through the merits of Jesus Christ, my Lord and Redeemer. *Amen.*

ACT OF LOVE

O my God, I love you above all things with my whole heart and soul, because You are all good and worthy of all my love. I love my neighbor as myself for love of You. I forgive all who have injured me, and I ask pardon of all whom I have injured. *Amen.*

ACT OF CONTRITION

O my God, I am heartily sorry for having offended You. I detest all my sins because of Your just punishments, but most of all because they offend You, my God, Who are all good and deserving of all my love. I firmly resolve, with the help of Your grace, to confess my sins, to do penance, and to amend my life. *Amen.*

PRAYER TO SAINT MICHAEL

Saint Michael the Archangel, defend us in battle. Be our protection against the wickedness and snares of the devil. May God rebuke him, we humbly pray, and do thou, O prince of the heavenly hosts, by the power of God, thrust into Hell Satan and all the evil spirits, who prowl about the world seeking the ruin of souls. *Amen.*

THE PRAYER OF FATIMA

O my Jesus, forgive us our sins, save us from the fires of Hell, and lead all souls into Heaven, especially those in most need of Thy mercy. *Amen.*

SPIRITUAL COMMUNION

My Jesus, as I cannot receive Thee now in the Most Holy Blessed Sacrament, I ask Thee to come into my heart, and make it like Thy heart. *Amen.*

PRAYER TO MY GUARDIAN ANGEL

Angel of God, my guardian dear,
To whom God's love commits me here,
Ever this day be at my side,
To light and guard, to rule and guide. *Amen.*

STATIONS OF THE CROSS

1. Jesus is condemned to death.
2. Jesus carries His Cross.
3. Jesus falls the first time.
4. Jesus meets His Mother.
5. Jesus is helped by Simon.
6. Veronica wipes the face of Jesus.
7. Jesus falls a second time.
8. Jesus speaks to the women.
9. Jesus falls a third time.
10. Jesus is stripped of His clothes.
11. Jesus is nailed to the Cross.
12. Jesus dies on the Cross.
13. Jesus is taken down from the Cross.
14. Jesus is placed in the tomb.

How have I acted toward God? Do I think of God and speak to Him by praying to Him each day?

Do I speak of God with reverence?

Do I go to Mass on Sunday?

Do I do all I can to make Sunday a day of rest and joy for my family?

Do I participate in Mass, or do I tease or distract others by laughing, talking, or playing?

Do I pay attention to my parents, priests, and teachers when they talk to me about God?

How have I acted toward others?

Do I obey my parents and teachers quickly and cheerfully, or must I be reminded many times?

Do I tell my parents or those in authority over me that I am sorry and ask them to forgive me when I have not minded them?

Do I obey the rules of my home and school?

Do I help my brothers, sisters, and classmates when they need my help?

Am I kind to everyone?

Did I hit, kick, or in any way hurt others on purpose?

Am I willing to play with everyone?

Did I make fun or say mean things to anyone?

Do I do all my classwork and my chores at home well?

Do I take care of my health by eating the right food, etc.?

Do I think or do bad things or say bad words?

Do I tell the truth?

Do I say things about other people that are not true?

Did I cheat in class or in a game?

Did I steal or keep things that are not mine?
Am I willing to share my things with others?
Do I return things that I have borrowed?

Art Credits

cover   *Resurrection of Lazarus* (detail), Fra Angelico, Scala/Art Resource, NY

8   *Madonna and Child Entrhoned with Saints* (detail), Raphael, Gift of J. Pierpont Morgan, Image © The Metropolitan Museum of Art

14   *Creation of the Animals*, Legouais, Erich Lessing/Art Resource, NY

18   *The Baptism of Christ* (detail), Perugino, Scala/Art Resource, NY

22   *The Expulsion from Eden*, Late Byzantine mosaic, ca. 1182–1192, Vanni/Art Resource, NY

26   *Angel Preventing the Sacrifice of Isaac*, Tiepolo, Scala/Art Resource, NY

32   *The Finding of Moses* (detail), Bourdon, Samuel H. Kress Collection, Image courtesy of the Board of Trustees, National Gallery of Art, Washington

36   *Scenes from the Life of Moses including Moses and the Tablets of the Law* (detail), Rosselli, Scala/Art Resource, NY

40   *David with the Head of Goliath*, Andrea del Castagno, Widener Collection, Image courtesy of the Board of Trustees, National Gallery of Art, Washington

46   *Angel in Adoration* (detail), Gozzoli, Scala/Art Resource, NY

54   *Holy Family*, Giulio Romano, Finsiel/Alinari/Art Resource, NY

58   *Annunciation* (detail), Filippo Lippi, Alinari/Art Resource, NY

64   *Way to Calvary* (detail), Tintoretto, Scala/Art Resource, NY

74   *The Adoration of the Shepherds*, Giorgione, Samuel H. Kress Collection, Image courtesy of the Board of Trustees, National Gallery of Art, Washington

78   *Baptism of Christ* (detail), Ghirlandaio, Scala/Art Resource, NY

82   *The Marriage at Cana*, Master of the Catholic Kings, Samuel H. Kress Collection, Image courtesy of the Board of Trustees, National Gallery of Art, Washington

88   *The Lord's Supper*, D. Bouts, Erich Lessing/Art Resource, NY

92   *The Crucifixion with Saint Jerome and Saint Francis*, Pesellino, Samuel H. Kress Collection, Image courtesy of the Board of Trustees, National Gallery of Art, Washington

98   *Deposition* (detail), Fra Bartolommeo, Nimatallah/Art Resource, NY

112   *Communion of the Apostles*, Fra Angelico, Nicolo Orsi Battaglini/Art Resource, NY

120   *Noli Me Tangere*, Duccio, Scala/Art Resource, NY

124   *The Descent of the Holy Spirit*, Bartholome Zeitbolm, Photograph courtesy of the National Gallery of Ireland

130   *Saint Augustine and the Child on the Seashore* (detail), Pinturicchio, Scala/Art Resource, NY

140   *The Assumption of the Virgin*, Michel Sittow, Ailsa Mellon Bruce Fund, Image courtesy of the Board of Trustees, National Gallery of Art, Washington

144   *Rose Window of the South Transept: The Wise and the Foolish Virgins*, Erich Lessing/Art Resource, NY

PHOTOGRAPHS: